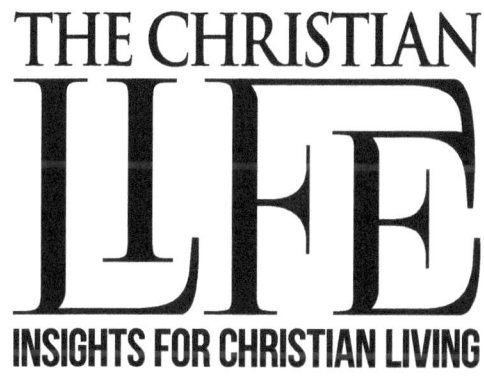

THE CHRISTIAN
LIFE

INSIGHTS FOR CHRISTIAN LIVING

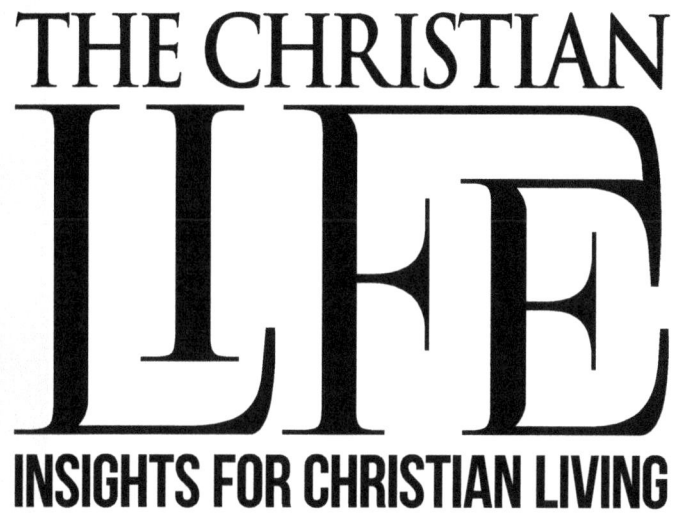

THE CHRISTIAN LIFE

INSIGHTS FOR CHRISTIAN LIVING

FATHER
CLETUS
CHUKWUDI
IMO

Imoklet Publishing

Copyright ©2023 Cletus Chukwudi Imo

Book and Cover Design - Kris VanDerVies | KMDezine Studio, California.

Paperback   ISBN 979-8-9891239-0-2
Hardback   ISBN 979-8-9891239-1-9

Printed in the United States of America.

I dedicate this book to
The Missionaries of the Lamb Foundation.

FOREWORD

By Fr. Innocent Emechete

*I*t is with pleasure that I write a Forward to *The Christian Life*. When Fr. Imo asked me to write a foreword to his book, I was very glad to do it because of the importance and potential of the book. The Title is appropriate and cogent for our time. It could not have come at a better time than now when Christians and particularly catholic Christians seem to be groping in the dark because of ignorance.

There are many Christians, but very, very few know what the Christian life is all about. The generation that had better training in the catechetics of Christianity and a thorough education on the Christian life seems to have disappeared. Many have died, and a big number of the remnant has been re-educated by new trends in society and religion. No wonder things have fallen apart, and the center can no longer hold. Societal ills of today can only be described in the superlative comparison as a result. The reason and technique of banding and handing down the Christian Faith have tremendously changed. The appropriate emphasis on what the Apostles handed down has undergone serious changes that make them sometimes unrecognizable for various reasons.

Who is to blame for this disconnect? One can hardly lay all the blame on the candidates for catechetical classes. Surely, they have a certain degree of the blame if and when they do not grasp the material and content of what was handed down to them or when they did not apply the teachings in their day-to-day lives. Sometimes people are raised in the Word of God, and later in life, they choose to deflect from their moral upbringing and follow the ways of the world.

But a greater blame seems to be on both the institution and their agents – the institution when it downgrades the standard to belong and look modern; the agents when they put more emphasis on themselves and what is in it for them at the expense of the message.

Sometimes, because of ignorance, they are not equipped to teach when they impose themselves on the institution for whatever reason.

It is for the above deficiencies in our practice of Christianity that Fr. Imo's book on *The Christian Life* is relevant. He broke it down to practicality of everyday life that everybody can understand and actualize. To make sure no one is tempted to call it his sentiment or opinion, he gave ample and robust quotations from the Word of God – *THE BIBLE*, to support every point. This author gave us the Christian life scaled down to easy and understandable everyday life in eight chapters. He started off with the notion that being Christians in *TRUTH* guarantees a saved life which is realizable through *GRACE* which is in itself a gift from God, when we have strong *FAITH* in God, strong *HOPE* in realizing His promises and *LOVE* for Him and for our neighbors. To achieve all this goal, Fr. Imo reminded us that *FORGIVENESS* of one another, having a life of *PRAYER* and *WORSHIP* rooted in the *SACRAMENTS*, are essential ingredients to achieve a saved life which is the ultimate goal.

This straight-forward, down-to-earth catechetical summary of the Christian Faith is an ideal read for every Christian and those who want to become one. It is not only foundational; it is also a refresher course in Christianity for practicing Christians because Christianity is a twenty-four-seven commitment. Essentially, it is a great tool for beginners and adults in RCIA programs. This book is in-depth as well as practical. Fr. Imo stumbled on it when he was faced with how to reach some people in his parish who were not in the parochial school catechetical program. He devised a gradual, step by step and comprehensive pedagogy online. It even grew bigger when the Covid-19 kept everybody locked down for about two years. I highly recommend it to everyone.

ACKNOWLEDGMENTS

vidence shows that no significant project is accomplished solo. This book represents some experiences that involve people and their faith interventions and questions about the life of the Church. Efforts have been made to take those thoughts and experiences shaped by dialogue and convey them in a simple and easy way to capture.

It is not easy to articulate all. However, to the Ever-Gracious God, be the praise, honor, and glory for the assistance and guidance in writing this book. To **Bishop Alberto Rojas** of the Diocese of San Bernardino, who believes that the love Christ "gives to all his children is all that any of us needs to achieve eternal life," I will always remain grateful for his love and care of the people of God.

I thank **Oje Imoohi,** a young Cal State University student, who asked the question that led to the writing of chapter one of this book. "Father, if Jesus died for our sins and saved us, why do we still go for confession and do penance?" Special thanks also go to my correspondence *catechism students,* past and present, who have been part of the circumstances that gave rise to the questions or part of helping me to think through the book—the *coordinators and catechists of St. John XXIII Catholic Community,* Fontana and Rialto.

I am most grateful to the *Family Intercessors of the Lamb members* with whom I have shared reflections, answered questions, and entertained interventions. Thanks to *Net Jay, Ryan Beck, Aurora and Max Soliguen* for their Christian love and charity. I thank *Phil Margala,* who reviewed the draft, raising issues and questions that compelled me to take a different and more productive path. Thanks also goes to *Fr. Innocent Emechete* who reviewed the script and wrote a foreword to the book, and to *Kris VanDerVies* who transformed the title and script into the beautiful book you are holding in your hands.

I especially thank my sister, *Anthonia Adiele,* whose faith and devotion influenced my early Christian life and commitment. Lastly, I thank my other siblings, *Anna, John, Luke, and Ignatius, their wives, husbands, and children,* whose relationships help challenge my Christian commitment. Thanks to the members of *Fr. Imo Faith-family, Family Intercessors of the Lamb,* and all whose support improved the form and content of this work.

TABLE OF CONTENTS

Do not be conformed to this
world, but be transformed by
the renewal of your mind, that
by testing you may discern what
is the will of God, what is good
and acceptable and perfect.

Romans 12:2

Christian Life

ife is one but lived at different levels based on motivations and personal values. While values form and inform a life, religious values do much more. Jesus came into the world to achieve religious values with a teaching and a way of life. "I have come that they may have life and have it in abundance" (Jn. 10:10b). This life is possible by following the life-giving message that Jesus taught and left for his Church. This life-giving message is about freedom from sin to realize an abundant life. In his teaching, Jesus revealed how human life has been decimated by sin (Jn. 8:34-36); ruled by Satan (Jn. 10:10a); and harassed by falsehood (Jn. 8:32). The life that Jesus gives is to be the fruit of a response to the words of life he preached (Jn. 6:63), and his sacrifice for salvation (Eph. 1:7).

With words, Jesus called the human person to knowledge, repentance from sin, faith in God, and love of God and neighbor. Those who accept this call and receive baptism in his name become not only children of God but Christians after the example of Christ.

Unfortunately, some believers do not know who they are in Christ as Christians. There are some misconceptions by which the term "Christian" is used today that are not at all consistent with what it means to be Christlike. Some who think Christianity is a religion of rules and laws believe that if one lives by high moral principles, they are surely Christian. For those who see Christianity as a religion of prayer, to pray is to be a Christian. For those who see it as a moral check with dos and don'ts to observe, to be law-abiding is to be a Christian. For those who see it as going to church, to attend church every Sunday is being a Christian. For those who see it as a problem-solving religion, to be a Christian is to have your problems solved. As a result, the Christian faith is not a matter of life, who we are in Christ, but what we do.

This book presents the simple teachings of Christ that show believers in Christ how to live the Christian life differently from the mere observance of laws. The commandments informed the Jews on how to live their life. While the values of the Jewish religion form and inform the life of the Jewish people, Jesus came and radicalized the commandments by inviting his disciples to live beyond the letter of the law. With this, he tells us that the life to which his disciples are called to live is a higher life.

The first objective of Christianity is, therefore, not problem-solving or a bundle of dos and don'ts but salvation and freedom of the person. When this is achieved, the believer then knows how to fight and solve problems. In this book, we strive to state that Christianity is a religion of life and love. God does not only create man in his own image to share in his dignity but also has a life that he wishes to share with humanity through his Son, Jesus Christ. This life of God is divine and grace-filled. Our sharing in it disposes us to discover and rediscover not only our divine dignity but the life such sharing calls us to live, namely, the life of grace, which disposes us to be full of the presence of God. It is the life Paul says is created after the likeness of God in Christ Jesus (Eph. 4:24).

This life is modeled on Jesus, who is the human personality of God who came to usher in the era of grace. As such, the Christian life entails following Jesus daily in his humility, grace, faith, love, forgiveness, and prayer. It is in this following of Jesus comes the name "Christian" (Acts 11:25-26). Jesus sets how to live this life by teachings that challenge the status quo. It is a life that is not ordinary, a life that calls for perspective change: love those who hate you (Lk. 6:27), turn the other cheek (Matt. 5:39), rejoice in your suffering, and "blessed" are the poor and the persecuted (Matt. 5:3). Give not only your coat (Lk. 3:11) but your very life (Matt. 16:25) for the sake of love.

It is this Christian lifestyle I have been sharing for some years now with some of my adult parishioners whose nature of work or studies makes it difficult to attend in-person catechism classes. As it were, when I was residing as a student priest at St. Peter and St. Paul Church, Alta Loma, I met some men and women who wanted to take classes in RCIA or Confirmation but could not because of time constraints. It was a bad feeling to see some of them who began classes but did not finish them because of their work or studies. The concern was enormous, but I could not do anything as a resident priest. However, immediately after finishing my studies and assigned to a parish, I started a Correspondence Catechism Class. It is now nine years in existence, and the testimonies of its results are evident in the parish. It is the fruit of the correspondence classes that grounds this book's reflections.

So, it is in an effort to demonstrate that the Christian is called to a set lifestyle that comes from a belief in Christ that this book is written.

It underscores that everything is not Christianity, and every life is not a Christian life. While there are many lifestyles, as there are many motivations and creeds, the Christian life is rich and unique. It is simple, noble, joyful, and rooted in the life of Christ. It is much more than honorific titles. Titles and hierarchies do not make a Christian.

That if you confess with your mouth, "Jesus is Lord," and believe in your heart that God raised him from the dead, you will be saved. For it is with your heart that you believe and are justified, and it is with your mouth that you confess and are saved.

Romans 10:9-10

CHAPTER 1

IT IS A
Saved Life

The Christian life is the product of the saving mystery of Christ. The salvation message has a history that begins with Genesis. The book of Genesis tells us that after the creation of Adam and Eve, God blessed them and said to them, "Be fruitful and multiply, and fill the earth and subdue it; and have dominion over the fish of the sea and over the birds of the air and over every living thing that moves upon the earth" (Gen. 1:28). God made our first parents stewards of his creation. He took great delight in them and provided them with the garden of Eden as a dwelling place (Gen. 22:8).

But when tested by the tempter, whom the Scripture calls the devil and Satan, they abused their freedom and disobeyed God. Satan tricked them into believing that they could be all-powerful and wise like God, on their own terms and conditions, according to their own desires and preferences (Gen. 3:4-6). Like Lucifer and the fallen angels who rebelled against God, Adam and Eve thought they could be equal with God and chart their own course for happiness and life together. They chose to believe

Satan's word over God's word, a choice that opened the door to sin, rebellion, and separation from God. In submitting to Satan, Adam and Eve became his subjects and gave up their dominion over the earth and its stewardship to him. In other words, tempted by the devil, the man let his trust in his Creator die in his heart and, abusing his freedom, disobeyed God's command. This fall resulted in a grievous wound that only God could heal and restore to wholeness.

The dominion Satan has achieved by his victory over Adam and Eve is what he bragged about when he took Jesus and showed him all the kingdoms of the world and said: "To you, I will give all this authority and their glory; for it has been delivered to me, and I give it to whom I will. If you, then, will worship me, it shall all be yours" (Lk. 4:5-7). While some writers say that Satan lied when he said that the kingdoms of the earth had been delivered to him, others say that he was talking about the stewardship of the earth, which Adam and Eve gave by their submission to him. The latter defend their stand by referring to the rule of Satan testified in the Scriptures. The extent of his rule is clearly indicated when he is called "the prince of this world" (12:31), "the prince of the power of the air" (Eph. 2:2), and "the god of this world" (2 Cor. 4:4). Even John says, "We know that we are of God, and the whole world is in the power of the evil one" (1 Jn. 5:19). He attributes this to the fact that "the old serpent, called the devil and Satan, deceived the whole world" (Rev. 12:9). The point we want to make here is that the sin of Adam and Eve gave power to Satan to have dominion over humanity.

What makes the failure of Adam and Eve an eternal disaster is that it corrupts their nature and is passed on to all human beings. The Catechism teaches us that; "By his sin, Adam lost the original holiness he received from God, not only for himself but for all human beings" (CCC. 403). With his sin, Adam afflicted all of us with a sin which is the "death of the soul." This is what Paul affirms when he says: "Sin came into the world through one man and death through sin, and so death spread to all men because all men sinned" (Rom. 5:12). In this way, the whole of human history is marked by the original fault freely committed by our first parents. The prohibition against eating "of the tree of knowledge of good and evil" spells out that "for in the day that you eat of it, you shall die" (Gen. 2:17). By this disobedience, death makes its entrance into human history (Rom. 5:12), confirming Paul's teaching that the wages of sin is death (Rom. 6:23). This death is not only physical but also spiritual.

In this interplay, Adam and Eve sold their freedom and willpower to Satan, and his authority began to reign over them. As a result of this, man's will is adversely affected. Jesus attributed man's impaired willpower to the lies of the devil. He revealed this when he was addressing the Pharisees: "You are from your father the devil, and you choose to do your father's desires. He was a murderer from the beginning and did not stand in the truth because there was no truth in him. When he lies, he speaks according to his nature, for he is a liar and the father of lies" (Jn. 8:44). This is to say that when Satan rules a man's will, he likes to do the will of Satan. "The Truth," Jesus said, "sets one free" (Jn. 8:32). If Satan is a liar, anyone who lives by his will, lives in lies and bondage without freedom until set free (Jn. 8:34). The implications of this situation abound: Man finds himself constrained to exercise his choice and action. He often refuses to acknowledge God as his beginning and disrupts his proper relationship with his ultimate goal. As a result, all of human life, whether individual or collective, shows itself to be a dramatic struggle between good and evil, light and darkness. In fact, man finds that by himself, he is incapable of battling the assaults of evil successfully so that everyone feels as though they are bound by chains (Gs. 13). Today, everyone is implicated by it and feels the overwhelming misery that oppresses us and our inclination toward evil and death.

The point here is that God created man in his own image and established him in his friendship - a friendship to be lived only in free submission to God. But when the devil seduced him to disobey God, all sin became disobedience to God. Consequently, the grace of original holiness was lost (Rom. 3:23). Unfortunately, psychologists think that sin results from inadequate social structures and human weakness. There is more to sin than the symptoms we experience daily. The Catechism teaches that sin is not a developmental flaw, a psychological weakness, a mistake, or the necessary consequence of an inadequate social structure (CCC. 387). In fact, the ultimate meaning of the power of sin is better understood only in the light of the death and resurrection of Christ. Satan is at the root of the symptoms of sin we see people commit. The human is engaged in a battle with the known and unknown (Eph. 6:10ff). Finding himself on this battlefield, man has to struggle to do what is right. The sin of Adam and Eve produced a human condition that makes humanity to be:

† subject to the authority of Satan and in need of freedom

† live in the bondage of sin and in need of salvation, and

† consigned to Sheol and eternal death and in need of eternal life

All these human conditions call for salvation.

WHAT JESUS DID TO SAVE US

As noted above, the actions of our first parents created a debt to be paid as a just demand of the law. In view of this, God started right from the beginning of the fall of our first parents to plan for human salvation. Genesis 3:9,15 gives us a picture of the first announcement of the Messiah and Redeemer, of a battle between the serpent and the woman, and of the final victory of a descendant of hers. The Church teaches that the unnamed woman in this text is Mary, and her seed who would bruise the serpent's head is Jesus. In line with human salvation, God used some Judges, kings, and prophets like Moses, David, Gideon, Samson, Isaiah, Jeremiah, Ezekiel, and John the Baptist to save Israel from physical death, consequences of sin, and the oppression of the devil during the years of waiting for the ultimate Messiah. But none of these could pay the debt incurred by the sin that disfigured humanity.

God did not leave humanity to their fate but promised to send them a Redeemer who would restore them and their descendants to the fullness of life with God. The prophet Isaiah foretold that God would send his people a Redeemer, born of a virgin mother from the house of David (Is. 7:14), who would willingly undergo affliction and chastisement to the point of shedding his blood to make atonement for their sins (Is. 53:1-12). Then at the appointed time, God sent his Son, Jesus Christ, who came to lift humanity from its fallen human nature at his own expense. Jesus came for this, confirmed it by his preaching and works, and surrendered himself to be crucified to save humanity at the appointed time. In the passion narrative, according to John, the last words that Jesus said on the Cross before he bowed his head and gave up the spirit were: "It is finished" (Jn. 19:30). This phrase is represented by one word in the original Greek, namely, "telestai" which means "paid in full." What is "finished" or "paid in full" is the debt we owe to God by our sins. This debt is specified in Romans 6:23, where Paul says that the wages of sin are death. What this means is that anyone who sins deserves to perish. This is why describing God's love, which saves us; John said: "For God so loved the world that he sent his only begotten son so that anyone who believes in him will not perish but have eternal life" (3:16).

The debt, therefore, we owe to God by our sin, by which we deserve to perish, is what Jesus says has been paid in full. Jesus does not, of course, only pay for the debt incurred by Adam and his descendants but for the individual sin we commit after Baptism. In other words, we are set free from original sin universally and from our sins when we repent and confess our sins. Our response to the work of Jesus makes us sons, not slaves, while our obedience to Satan makes us slaves, not sons. In this way, we discover that freedom is not only possible, but to be a Christian is to be free.

As descendants of Adam and Eve, each person, before the death of Jesus, carried the mark of death due to sin and was liable to eternal damnation with no hope of heavenly glory. This is a fact of the human person, which Paul confirmed when he said that the wages of sin is death. But as part of human redemption, Jesus descended into Sheol (Hades) during his death and took three days to proclaim the Good News of salvation to the dead held captive by Satan (Matt. 27:52-53). Having paid the debt owed to God by our sins, Jesus had the power and authority to break loose from the chains of death over him and liberate the dead whom Satan held in captivity (Rom. 3:15; 1 Cor. 15:20; Heb. 13:20).

The dead in Sheol were deprived of the vision of God – both bad and righteous people - while waiting for the Redeemer. Jesus went into the depths of death so that "the dead will hear the voice of the son of God and those who hear will live" (Jn. 5:25; Matt. 12:40; Rom. 16:7; Eph. 4:9). Jesus, the author of life, by dying destroyed "him who has the power of death, that is, the devil, and delivered all those who through fear of death were subject to lifelong bondage" (Heb. 2:14-15; Acts 3:15). This battle is what he meant when he told John, "I am the first and the last, the one who lives. Once I was dead, but now I am alive forever and ever. I hold the keys to death and the netherworld" (Rev. 1:17b-18). This is how Jesus won a victory over the devil.

As we can see, in his passion, Jesus defeated the devil and, by his victory, became lord to reign for those delivered from the authority and dominion of Satan (Matt. 28:20). Rising up from the grave, he greeted his disciples: "Be of good cheer for I have overcome the world" (Jn. 16:33). By overcoming the One who is called the father of this world, Jesus became victorious over the world. He fulfilled what he said at the early part of his ministry: "I have come that you may have life and have it in abundance" (Jn. 10:10). And with his life given in exchange for our life, we become subjects of eternal life which of course begins in this life. Jesus paid with his life for this abundant life for us to enjoy here and hereafter.

This priceless act of the grace of his passion took an unquantified toll on Jesus. It cost Jesus his life by dying to give us life; it cost him his sanctity and holiness for being made sin on our behalf who knew no sin (2 Cor. 5:21). Jesus was tortured with the worst form of death and suffered deep anguish and pains. His nerves were pierced with extraordinary nails. He was stripped of his clothes and is shamefully made fun of by passersby and the authorities of Israel. He was ridiculed for his power, ridiculed about his purpose, and ridiculed about his identity. He accepted the cup of our sin and our suffering and drank it to the bitter dregs. What a heroic death! What extravagant love! What a grace! What salvation!

In all this, Jesus bears witness in his own person and in the mighty works which he performed that God's deliverance has truly come to those who accept him as Savior and Lord. With all this, Jesus saved and restored us to our former identity as those "created in the image of God for good works" (Eph. 2:10). In this, we are delivered from the authority and dominion of Satan over us, sin, and its wrath, eternal death and the darkness of hell. Our salvation through the work of Jesus Christ is an accomplished reality universally. For now, we are still being saved (1 Cor. 1:18) and will be saved at the end of time. The future of our salvation is what we look forward to at the end of our life. With this, we await salvation that takes place in the believer's future, which Paul says is near (Rom. 13:11) and exhorts us to work it out with fear and trembling (1 Thess. 5:8).

IF JESUS DIED FOR OUR SINS, WHY DO WE GO FOR CONFESSION?

Jesus paid in full the debt Adam and Eve incurred and shared with us. We participate in the grace of this endowment by undergoing a Baptism. Baptism is the sacrament that lays the foundation of our Christian life in Christ. At the beginning of his ministry, Jesus received Baptism from John the Baptist. But when he came up for baptism, John saw this as inappropriate for the One he knew to be the spotless Lamb of God, but Jesus replied, "Let it be so now, for thus it is fitting for us to fulfill all righteousness" (Matt. 3:15). What kind of "righteousness" does Jesus want to fulfill? Righteous living is a legal requirement that one fulfills by undertaking some ritual ordinances like Circumcision, Baptism, keeping the Passover feast, and others. The fulfillment of these would make one a true Jew.

To become a true Jew, Jesus must undertake Baptism and observe the Sabbath ritual purification. Though the fulfillment of all these ordinances would lead to human righteousness, which is defective, Jesus fulfilled them to transform human righteousness into his own righteousness. Though Jesus knew no sin, "God made him to be sin on our behalf, that we might become the righteousness of God in him" (2 Cor. 5:21) through his perfect righteousness. In this way, Jesus becomes our perfect substitute so that in him we may become the righteousness of God.

In his baptism on the Cross (Lk. 12:50), Jesus takes our sins and gives us his righteousness. In so doing, he kicks off the era of grace. He inaugurated the salvation he accomplished on the Cross on his baptism at the Jordan. Through our Baptism we begin to participate in the righteousness brought by his work of salvation. We begin to live eternal life through the life of grace. Eternal life is to be understood as sharing in the life of God (Jn. 1:4). As Jesus became part of the righteousness of humanity to live their lives, we are to become part of his own righteousness to live his life. This is what our baptism bequeaths us. The eternal life we enjoy now assures us of the eternal bliss waiting for us at the end of life.

All this is possible through Baptism in which we are buried with Christ and raised from it to a new life, a new status, a new vision, a new faith, a new hope, and a new identity. Those who are in Christ Jesus are a new creation (2 Cor. 5:17). This new birth is the fruit of a transformation that opens the door to seeing reality from a divine point of view when enlightened by the Holy Spirit. This is why Jesus said that we must be born from above – empowered from above (Jn. 3:3; Acts 1:8) to be able to live the life of grace. This then conveys the idea that people are without life until they receive the divine gift, which can be received and experienced in the present. Through Baptism we receive the very breath of heaven that fills our hearts with God's Spirit and enlivens our feeble arms and weak knees (Heb. 12:12) to "run the race set before us" (Heb. 12:1).

Our baptism in the death and resurrection of Jesus saved us from the power of sin. However, our freedom is not taken away from us. God gave us the freedom to choose what is right and pleasing to his kingdom. If we misuse it, we offend God and become the slaves of Satan. This is why we are held accountable for our personal sins. Though Jesus provided us with the Sacrament of Reconciliation as a remedy for personal sins, the abuse of our freedom is a sign of irresponsibility, a deviation from the life of the spirit. Our salvation is not a license to live in sin but freedom and grace to live above sin. Sins do not just cease to exist by our baptism or confession of them. We have to do something. The traditional clarion call to bridle our appetites and numb our sensibilities through mortification and self-denial is a must if we want to be free from the hold of sin. As a matter of fact, you cannot belong to Christ Jesus unless you crucify all self-indulgent passions and desires (Gal. 5:24). As Paul puts it, "For if you live according to the flesh you will die, but if by the Spirit you put to death the deeds of the body you will live" (Rom. 8:13). Christians are the children of light. However, they abuse their freedom and state of grace any time they walk in the darkness of sin. To maintain our state of grace, we are to Christianize our desires by allowing the Christian virtues to occupy our minds. We should desire the will of God and allow it to prevail over our will. "For God is at work in you, both to will and to work for his good pleasure" (Phil. 2:13). We should make our will the servant of the will of God.

Sin is a battle that every believer must intentionally fight without any reservations. We must confront our desires, feelings, and anything that takes our attention. This is important because our desires determine our attention to something. If we desire peace, we will listen and understand the language of peace. If we desire Christian values, the voice of God in the Bible will appeal to us. So, we need an intimate relationship with God to be able to distinguish his voice from the many voices of the darkness of sin that influence our values and behaviors. The human person, by nature, has the ability to choose good or bad. If we are sincere and aware of how we behave, we will discover that each one of us has the potential for both good and bad. There is part of us that loves, part of us that hates, part of us that makes peace, and part of us that revolts. There is part of us that resents and part of us that cooperates. There is part of us that builds and part of us that destroys. My desire to be free from sin will be determined by which part I feed or starve, which I enthrone or dethrone when reacting to lies, truths, and life challenges.

Because the Holy Spirit within us needs to have a full grasp of every aspect of our being to operate adequately in our lives, we need to surrender our lives totally to God. If we do not surrender our self-will to the will of God, two wills or powers will be at work in us at the same time. The grace of our salvation will endure if we allow the life of God within us to grow and shine forth. Then if we desire and pray for the willpower that comes from God and fails to receive it, our disposition is not right. To ask for God's will is to place him in charge of our lives and actions, which calls for self-surrender.

In our Baptism, God gave us his spirit to help us live godly. When this is done, and the Holy Spirit begins to rule in our lives, we will realize that when we sin, it is not a sin against the letter of the law or the commandments but against a person, the person of God. Those who walk by the spirit do not desire sin or deliberately will to commit sin because it offends

God. While those who walk in the flesh do whatever helps them achieve their desires and do not consider how it affects God. Through the light of the Holy Spirit, we will see ourselves the way we are, how much our love for God has been impaired by our sins, and the need to seek reconciliation with God who has been offended and hurt. This means that to enjoy the freedom and steady victory over sin, we are to walk by the Spirit" (Eph. 5:18). The only way to act righteously is to be filled with and moved by the Holy Spirit. For us, "it is not by Might, nor by Power, (that we win) but by my Spirit, says the Lord" (Zech. 4:6).

The sequel to this is living out the resurrection power of Jesus in our lives. Resurrection is the assurance that new life is possible (2 Cor. 5:17). The new life of resurrection is not automatic but the result of death. The paradox is that death leads to life. When we die to ourselves, we rise to new life in Christ. The good news is that resurrection becomes our way of living after our baptismal death of being buried with Christ. We subject ourselves to death whenever we sin by dying to sin and rising to new life. To die to oneself is to put to death what is sinful in a person. All we can do now to be raised with Christ and to be free from sin is to be dead to the world, to fear, to self, to superstitions, to live for Satan, and begin to live for Jesus in all things.

IF JESUS HAS SAVED US, WHY DO WE STILL EXPERIENCE THE THREAT OF SATAN?

One of the riches of God we celebrate during Lent is the defeat of Satan by Jesus Christ and our freedom as redeemed children of God. However, some believers in Christ still wonder what it means to celebrate the freedom of our redemption since the devil still harasses Christians and non-Christians alike. As we have already noted, Jesus has delivered us from the dominion of Satan. In the wilderness, Jesus was tempted by the devil but overcame his antics. His death and resurrection defeated Satan's hold on humanity and set us free. He disarmed the devil, stripped him, and made a show of him openly on our behalf. Paul puts it thus: "Even when you were dead in sin, and your flesh was uncircumcised, God gave you new life in company with Christ. He pardoned all our sins. He canceled the bond that stood against us with all its claims, snatching it up and nailing it to the Cross. Thus, did God disarm the principalities and powers. He made a public show of them and, leading them off captive, triumphed in the person of Christ" (Col. 2:13-15).

This defeat of the devil by Jesus marked phase one of God's plan for the devil. The elimination of the devil has two phases. Phase one is about his defeat and dethronement, and phase two is about his everlasting banishment from the earth. While phase one took place with the first coming of Christ, phase two will happen during the second coming of Christ. With phase one defeat, Satan does not have authority over humanity as he had before the coming of Christ. He is no longer lord and master. Instead, Jesus, who defeated and won our freedom from Satan by his obedience to God, is now our Lord and Master (Phil. 8:9-10).

It is important to note that even though Satan has been defeated and dethroned, he has not been destroyed. He still exists with limited powers. This is why he is still tireless at work, tempting and accusing us day and night before our God (Rev. 12:10). Peter envisions the devil as prowling around like a roaring lion looking for someone to devour, and exhorts us to stand up to him, strong in faith (1 Pt. 5:8). This is to be taken seriously because "spiritual warfare is a reality." Every Christian is engaged in a battle of some sort, either against the devil, sin, or the world spiritually, physically, and mentally.

Unfortunately, some things we do create openings in our lives and make us vulnerable to satanic attacks. To be able to fight with victory over Satan, we should have nothing to do with the works of iniquity and impurity, consulting of oracles and seeking the services of soothsayers, reading of stars and palms, spilling of blood, possession of talismans, living in unforgiveness, living in sin, living an amoral life or living in doubt and fears about the existence of God. These things make us susceptible to the attacks of and partnership with Satan.

It is true that the devil still has some powers; this should not call for any anxiety at all. This is so because Jesus has empowered us by his crucifixion and resurrection to engage in spiritual warfare with victory. Today we have the authority of the Children of God to trample over Satan and his agents. "Go into all the world and preach the gospel to the whole creation. Whoever believes and is baptized will be saved, but whoever does not believe will be condemned. And these signs will accompany those who believe: in my name, they will cast out demons; they will speak in new tongues; they will pick up serpents with their hands; and if they drink any deadly poison, it will not hurt them; they will lay their hands on the sick, and they will recover" (Mk. 16:15-18). This is realized today by both priests and the lay faithful who know their God-given power and how to employ such in prayer through faith. As such, we are no longer to be afraid of Satan. As Paul puts it: "You are of God, my little children, and have overcome them: *because greater is he that is in you than he that is in the world*". Our job now is to strive through faith and good works to realize our power over Satan and use it against him to dismantle his activities.

Paul has much to say about spiritual warfare, and in his letter to the Ephesians, he gives us certain tools we can use to fight the devil: the sword of the spirit (word of God), the shield of faith, the breastplate of righteousness, truthful life and peace with all (Eph. 6:10-15). Jesus has left us with the example of how he defeated the devil through his expert knowledge of the Scriptures during his temptation (Lk. 4:1-13) by allowing his religious convictions to influence his actions. He overcame his temptations because he desired to do the will of God (Jn. 4:31). Joshua is right when he says that familiarity with the Scriptures delivers us from temptation and wrongdoing (Jos. 1:8) and opens the door to success.

It is important to note that spiritual warfare is fought in the spirit and not in the flesh. This is part of why God poured his spirit into us to enable us to pray in the spirit and fight the battle of faith against the devil. Success comes when we fight the devil with Jesus, the victorious One, and this depends on our relationship with God. Anyone who fights the devil in the flesh is subject to failure, if not destruction. It is not by might or power that the mountain will move but by my spirit, says the Lord (Zech. 4:6). Therefore, fan into flame the gifts of the spirit you received when hands were laid upon you against the wiles of the enemy (2 Tim. 1:6).

The central message is that the threat of Satan can be overcome by Christians who, believing in the power and victory of Jesus, fight in faith with and through Jesus. With Jesus, the threat of the devil does not intimidate us anymore. Before the work of salvation, Satan has authority over humanity due to the wages of the sin of Adam and Eve. But since Jesus paid our debt fully due to sin, Jesus has empowered us by his victory to enjoy the freedom of the redeemed and to participate in his victory over

Satan. He has taught us to have, as our priority, the willingness to do the will of God and to use the words of the Scriptures to diffuse the devil's deceit in the strength of the Holy Spirit. Today we have the power to deal with Satan if we walk by the spirit under the Lordship of Jesus Christ. We can do this effectively if nothing in our possession belongs to the devil. We are truly saved, threat notwithstanding!

OUR SALVATION IS REAL

At Christmas, we celebrate the birth of our salvation in Jesus Christ, but on Easter, we celebrate the certainty of this salvation. The Bible uses three tenses to describe our salvation:

† We have been saved as an event in the past.

† We are being saved as a present event.

† We will ultimately be saved as an event in the future.

This does not mean three types of salvation but three dimensions of the same salvation wrought by Jesus Christ. As it were, the Lord Jesus Christ has saved us from eternal punishment caused by the sin of our first parents (Eph. 2:5,8; 2 Tim. 1:9; Tit. 3:5). As a past reality, we all have been saved from the hold and bondage of sin, and dominion and lordship of Satan. This is what we celebrate on Good Friday. Jesus has fully paid the debt for our redemption with his life. We begin to share in it the moment we accept Jesus and are baptized. All that is required from us is faith in what he has done and to lay claim to it as beneficiaries.

This brings us to salvation as a present reality (1 Cor. 1:18, 15:1-2; 2 Cor. 2:15). We are indeed saved, but because we are humans, we engage in a daily battle that puts our salvation to challenge and calls for our being saved daily. As humans, today we are victorious, but tomorrow we fail; today we are strong, but tomorrow we become weak. With his lofty promises, tactics, and deceit, the devil prowls around like a roaring lion looking for someone to devour and repossess. So, any time we submit ourselves to sin and Satan, we lose our freedom and stand to be delivered from the bondage of the sin in question and be reconciled to the Lord. As saved sons and daughters of God, it is our duty to avoid anything that has to do with the things from which we have been saved, namely, sin and the devil. Jesus saved us from the dominion of sin through his obedience to God. We are expected to participate in the obedience of Jesus and thus give sin and Satan no opportunity to enslave us. In addition to the many tools Jesus has given us to fight the daily battle over sin and Satan, he left us the Sacrament of Reconciliation to help us when we fail. When this happens, we repent, confess our sins, and are forgiven by the good lord. This struggle to retain the salvation Jesus has already given us is what is meant by being saved. As a result, Paul exhorts us to work out our salvation with fear and trembling (Phil. 2:12).

Salvation as a future reality (Rom. 5:9; Thess. 5:9-10, 1 Pt. 1:5) is the one which everyone works towards as a final destiny. Often, we emphasize this salvation from the damnation of one's soul at the end of life at the detriment of the other dimensions (Acts 16:30-31). In pursuit of what to do to go to heaven or earn eternal life, we fail to realize we have been saved and are being saved so that we will never be found wanting at the end of life. In fact, that we will be saved is a journey that is already in process. Let us, therefore, conduct ourselves as those who have been redeemed by living above board in our daily undertakings and not have anything to do with the works of darkness and iniquity (Eph. 5:11).

CONCLUSION

As we can see, from the scriptural point of view, salvation is a process that begins when a person first becomes a Christian and continues through the rest of his life, and finally concludes at the Final Judgment. We are saved, we are being saved, and we will be saved. We celebrate the certainty of this three-faceted gift of God on Easter. The resurrection of Jesus demonstrates our salvation as a time-tested reality founded on solid grounds.

In this way, we are consoled by the certainty that Jesus did not only die but has risen and lives with the Father and with us (Matt. 28:19). By his death, he has redeemed us from the curse of the law by becoming a curse for us (Gal. 3:13) and in the process reconciled us in his fleshly body through death in order to present us holy and blameless and above reproach before him (Col. 1:22). By his resurrection he has caused us to live in the hope of resurrection (1 Pt. 1:3). Now he lives forever, and holds the key to yesterday, today, and tomorrow. In our suffering, he suffers with us; in death, he dies with us and lives on in glory with us. Now we do not let our hearts be troubled (Jn. 14:1) because our hopes are not broken but fulfilled. Our future is not destroyed but perfected. Our life is not in danger but secured for all eternity. This way, we live in the hope that is not vague, in the hope that gives certainty and courage to face the future. This makes tolerable the sufferings of the present moment, which are not comparable to the future glory (Rom. 8:18). Today, like Paul, we live and trust that Christ's grace is enough for us (2 Cor. 12:9), and the power of his resurrection is our door to new life (Phil. 3:10).

As a result, every Easter we celebrate how we are saved by rising with Christ from the grave of sin to a new life of grace. In so doing, we enter the life of God as we turn to a new way of thinking and acting with Christ.

We celebrate how the victory of Jesus becomes our victory, and his rising becomes our rising from the lure and enslavement of sin. In other words, we rise from our old way of life to a new way of life, from doing our will to doing God's will, from a selfish lifestyle to a selfless lifestyle, and from being mere nominal Christians to being committed Christians. In other words, the resurrection paradox is that death leads to life. When we die to ourselves, we rise to new life in Christ. To die to oneself is to put to death what is sinful in a person. The good news is that the resurrection of Christ is now our way of living after our baptismal death of being buried with Christ. Saved by grace from the grave of sin, we strive to be dead to the world and to live for the Lord in all things. This is what it means to be saved, to be a Christian.

For by grace you have been saved through faith. And this is not your own doing; it is the gift of God, not a result of works, so that no one may boast. For we are his workmanship, created in Christ Jesus for good works, which God prepared beforehand, that we should walk in them.

Ephesians 2:8-9

CHAPTER 2

IT IS A LIFE OF
Grace

Christianity is a religion of grace. It is grace that differentiates it from other religions of the world. Grace is God's "riches" made possible to humanity through the death of Jesus Christ. It is God's free gift to his people to help boost our state of holiness, goodness, and well-being. We ask for God's grace each time we pray because we believe that grace enables us to do things well. We pledge to be able to do something by grace when we say: "By God's grace, I shall conquer." "By his grace, I will be all right." We sing it in our songs, as in the case of the popular "Amazing Grace" by John Newton.

Grace is not earned by human achievement but given by God. It can be given as forgiveness to remit sin, mercy in place of punishment, love for the delinquent, or salvation from bondage. As a gracious God, he is not only rich in mercy, love, and forgiveness; it is who he is as he said of himself in the book of Exodus, "The Lord, the Lord, a God merciful and gracious, slow to anger, and abounding in steadfast love and faithfulness, keeping steadfast love for thousands, forgiving iniquity and transgression and sin, yet by no means clearing the guilty, but visiting the iniquity of the parents upon the children and the children's children, to the third and the fourth generation" (Ex. 34:6-7). In this revelation of his identity, God tells us that goodness, love, and mercy are personal manifestations of his nature.

Therefore, God does not hesitate to invite us to a state of grace: "Oh, come to the water all you who are thirsty, though you have no money. Come! Why spend money on what is not bread, your wages on what fails to satisfy? Listen, listen to me, and you will have good things to eat and rich food to enjoy. Pay attention, come to me; listen, and your soul will live. With you, I will make an everlasting covenant because of my sure, steadfast love." (Is. 55:1-3). This invitation to a Covenant of love is God's way of giving freely to boost our life and makeup what we lack.

In Old Testament, grace is manifested through divine favors. There are various instances where God makes his grace available by giving his love, mercy, healing, forgiveness, or favors freely to his people, unmindful of their unfaithfulness and ingratitude. For instance, when God was not happy about man's wickedness on earth (Gen. 6:5), he spelled out punishment, but Noah found "favor in the eyes of the Lord" (Gen. 6:8) and was spared. Is it any wonder why the author of the book of Lamentations, filled with awe at the magnitude of God's wealth of graciousness, exclaimed: "The steadfast love of the Lord never ceases, his mercies never come to an end; they are new every morning; great is thy faithfulness" (3:22-23).

In the New Testament, these "riches" of God are made available to the disciples through Jesus, who is God's love for humanity. This began when God took human nature by parceling himself as a gift into the womb of Mary. "And the Word became flesh and dwelt among us, full of grace and truth; we have beheld his glory, glory as of the only Son from the Father" (Jn. 1:14).

By taking a human form, the grace of the remission of sin is made available in the person of Jesus. He came over-flowing with the grace of God. In Jesus, God enters the union and communion of life with the human person. He is the saving grace of God to the world. "For God so loved the world that he gave his only Son so that everyone who believes in him may not perish but may have eternal life" (Jn. 3:16). Humanity assumes divinity and begins to share and partake in the divine nature of his presence and powers. "And from his fullness have we all received, grace upon grace" (Jn. 1:16). One work of God's grace build upon another work of his grace and begins to mark the ministry of Christ.

Throughout his ministry, Jesus made God's favors available through preaching, healing, forgiving, and feeding the poor. But by dying on the cross to pay for our sins, the highest point of love and sacrifice, Jesus ushered in the era of grace and raised the human person to the status of sharing in divine nature (2 Pt. 1:4) which enables us to live a life that reflects God's holy nature. Grace becomes the means of sharing in God's life and riches at the expense of Christ. Then to be a Christian is to share in grace. Paul describes it thus: "But because of his great love for us, God, who is rich in mercy, made us alive with Christ even when we were dead in transgressions. God raised us up with Christ and seated us with him in the heavenly realms in Christ Jesus, in order that in the coming ages, he might show us the incomparable riches of his grace, expressed in his kindness to us in Christ Jesus. For it is by grace you have been saved, through faith, and that not from yourselves. It is a gift of God, not of works so that no one can boast" (Eph. 2:4-9). What love; what a precious gift!

The place of grace will be appreciated if we examine the struggles of the human person to live right and please God before Jesus came to the scene. Genesis account tells us that God created the world in perfect harmony and peace and said that everything is good. This good world did not last long. For a little while, sin came in, and evil's door let loose (Gen. 3:14). The darkness of sin was scattered all over the face of the earth. The reason for all this is human nature. It is this human condition that Isaiah speaks about when he says that man's righteous acts are like filthy rags" before a holy God (Is. 64:6). The same is true of Jeremiah, who says that "man's heart is deceitful and desperately wicked" (Jer. 17:9). Hence every effort to please God is made difficult if not impossible.

In the face of the rising and falling of God's children due to sin and the inability to please God in Old Testament relationships, God did not overlook or abandon his children to drown in sin. In their powerlessness, God always came to their rescue, reviving and aiding them with mercy, love, and forgiveness. He showed favors through human Messiahs like Samson, Gideon, Samuel, prophets, and John the Baptist. He provided the people with favors through celebrations that made his riches available: feasts, ceremonies, prayers, and ritual observances. He also gave them his law to enable them to perform righteous deeds before him. But over time, the rabbis developed a list of 613 separate laws: 148 commands and 365 prescriptions, and in the process, it became extremely difficult to keep the law completely or achieve true righteousness in so doing.

As man could not achieve righteousness by all that he does, God chooses to come to live with humanity, putting on our human nature. He did this to teach us how to be faithful in our nature as humans with the aid of his grace through Baptism. All the efforts God made in the Old Testament to help his people to live good lives and be in the right relationship with him came to fulfillment in Jesus, the love of God who came to share his life with us. In Jesus Christ, then, God shows himself as the true engineer of the universe, who has come to repair what sin has destroyed and empower humanity with grace at his own expense. For in Jesus dwells all the goodness of God's kingdom and all the fullness of God in a human form.

JESUS'S WORK OF GRACE

Jesus is God made man. As God incarnate, he is the bearer of God's favors and riches. Paul tells the Colossians that "Jesus Christ is the dwelling place of God's glory in whom all the fullness of the Deity lives in bodily form" (Col. 2:9). Through the Incarnation of Jesus, God's presence took our human form, and dwelt among us. This is very explicit in how Jesus revealed himself to Philip: "Anyone who has seen me has seen the Father" (Jn. 14:9). So, Christ is the visible manifestation of God. In him dwells fully the riches of God.

Jesus came to the earth to make God's riches available to humanity. To bring about redeeming grace, he had to do so at his own expense to atone for the debt incurred by the sin of our first parents. This took a painful journey in which he gave up his life to be immortalized to allow humanity to share in divine nature (2 Pt. 1:4) through divine righteousness. This is to be done by his suffering and death. At the appointed time, Jesus was falsely accused and condemned to die by crucifixion. While his torturers thought they were putting an end to his life, they did not know that their wicked action would be a blessing in disguise.

Jesus did not hesitate to surrender himself to the Jews to be crucified (Jn. 19:30).

On the cross, his side was pierced, and from it came water and blood, a symbol of cleansing and sanctification. When he gave up his spirit, he said: "It is finished." The debt and its just demand are paid, completely satisfied, and finished. In this exclamation, he expressed how his death has satisfied the just demand of the debt due to sin by humanity. He thus accomplished the work that paid for the debt completely; no addition, no subtraction. This accomplished work on the cross at Calvary gave birth to grace. His sacrifice opened the door for an entirely different kind of life, where grace becomes our heavenly resource for progressive practical growth in godliness.

This priceless act of grace of his passion took an unquantified toll on Jesus. It cost Jesus his life by dying to give us life. It cost him his sanctity and holiness for being made to be sin on our behalf who knew no sin (2 Cor. 5:21). Jesus was tortured with the worst form of death and suffered deep anguish and pain. He was stripped of his clothes and shamefully made fun of by passersby, chief priests, scribes, elders, and one of the thieves. He was ridiculed for his power, his purpose, and his identity. He accepted the cup of our sin and suffering and drank it to the bitter dregs. What a heroic death! What extravagant love! What a work of grace! In this, Jesus personally bears witness in his own person and in the mighty works, he performed that the era of grace has come.

In doing the work that brought us grace, he surrendered himself and undertook the path of his passion, the expense he had to pay to save humanity. In this selfless sacrifice, Jesus broke the chains of selfishness that characterize our human nature. In his obedience, he shows us how to choose what gives God glory and how to desire to do the will of God. Jesus has not only made this choice possible but has also given us the power to make it. The selfless choice demonstrated by Abraham in giving his son, Isaac, to God's will, Jesus perfected by the self-giving of himself freely and selflessly to God's will. In other words, this act of his is God's free gift made available to the whole world at his own expense. It is in essence, the free and unmerited gift of God given to all who exercise faith in Christ and his redemption.

GRACE AND BAPTISM

Grace opens the door closed by sin and makes man acceptable to his Creator, who is all good. For us to share in grace, we must undergo the rite of baptism to die with Jesus to sin and rise with him to new life. In so doing, we begin to participate in the righteousness of Jesus brought by his work of salvation. We begin to live eternal life through the life of grace. Eternal life is sharing in the life of God. "In him was life, and the life was the light of all people" (Jn. 1:4). Eternal life is the abundant life that Jesus came to give to believers (Jn. 10:10), and which we participate in through faith in Jesus. It is a participation in the life of grace.

So, the life of grace begins with Baptism. Jesus referred to it when Nicodemus came privately at night to seek a private and undisturbed conversation with him (Jn. 3:3-5).

When Nicodemus met with Jesus, he asked a question that came from the very heart of the Mosaic law: "How can one get right with God and enter God's kingdom?" Jesus' answer was brief and startling: "Unless one is born anew, he cannot see God" (Jn. 3:3).

The new birth that Jesus spoke about here is not a physical birth but a spiritual birth that is completely new and radical and comes from God himself. Jesus said that this rebirth was necessary if one was to enter God's kingdom. In his difficulty in understanding how this would be possible, Jesus explained that this change could only come about through the work and action of the Holy Spirit. This rebirth in the Spirit is very real and experiential, like the wind that can be felt and heard while it is invisible to the eyes. It marks how the human person can, by faith, be infused with grace and attain the righteousness that makes him please God. It is not surprising that Jesus asked John to baptize him to fulfill all righteousness (Matt. 3:13-15). In Baptism, Jesus transforms us into himself and elevates us to the level of sharing in his divine grace and righteousness.

It is important to note that before now, baptism was one of the ways a person is made right before God. As one who took flesh from Mary, Jesus received baptism to righteously identify with other Jewish worshipers and be acceptable to God. He accepted to undergo baptism by John the Baptist, not because he needed human righteousness, but to identify with it to transform human righteousness into his own righteousness. It is part of the work of Jesus to transform human righteousness. In other words, he did it in view of his second baptism on the cross. Speaking about the death which he was going to undergo to save us and usher in the era of grace, Jesus said to his disciples: "But I have a baptism to be baptized with, and how great is my distress until it is accomplished" (Lk. 12:50). This passage is a reference to his passion on the cross. The salvation which he accomplished on the cross was inaugurated at his baptism in the River Jordan. It was in this baptism that he was made to be sin on our behalf so that we might become "the righteousness of God in him" (2 Cor. 5:21) through his perfect righteousness. In this way, Jesus becomes our perfect substitute so that in him we may become the righteousness of God. In other words, in his baptism, Jesus takes our sin and gives us his righteousness. Just as Jesus became part of the righteousness of humanity to live our lives, we are to become part of his own righteousness to live his life through baptism. In fact, what Christ is by nature, we become by grace. God is no longer for us, just the Almighty out there or perhaps a seemingly impersonal "God." He is Abba, my Father! A personal Father, God!

This new life of baptism brings us into an experiential relationship with God as his adopted sons and daughters (Rom. 6:4; 8:10-11). This life of grace builds on, sanctifies, and elevates our human nature to the status of divine adoption. This new life in the Spirit brings us into God's kingdom of righteousness, peace, and joy (Rom. 14:17). "But when the goodness and loving kindness of God our Savior appeared, he saved us, not because of any works of righteousness that we had done, but according to his mercy, through the water of rebirth and renewal by the Holy Spirit" (Tit. 3:4-5).

A person who is thus baptized by accepting Jesus as Lord and Savior in the early Church is said to be justified. Grace is the reason for justification before God. It is by the power of the grace of Baptism that believers are justified. Justification happens at the moment when one submits in faith to Jesus Christ. Justification is the act of God in which sinners who confess their faith in Jesus Christ are declared innocent as if they had never sinned. The change of heart exercised through repentance, baptism, and believing the Gospel is marked by the penitent receiving baptism and the gift of the Holy Spirit. It is a free gift of God's grace based entirely on the merits of our Lord Jesus Christ on the Cross of Calvary. Peter told them, "Repent and be baptized every one of you in the name of Jesus Christ so that your sins may be forgiven, and you will receive the gift of the Holy Spirit" (Acts 2:38). In other words, justification as part of grace is not salvation. One problem that Luther had, and many Christians still have, is confusing justification with salvation. They are not the same. While justification marks the beginning of belief in Christ, salvation is a past event that has a present and a future reality.

GRACE AND SALVATION

The work of salvation is accomplished by Jesus on the cross of Calvary. This work that Jesus undertakes to save us is what ushers in the grace that saves us. He alone did this work. In other words, salvation is possible only by grace. It is not what we have done or the merits of good deeds but the love of God. "For God so loved the world that he gave his only Son so that everyone who believes in him may not perish but may have eternal life" (Jn. 3:16). This great work of the Lord calls for faith. It takes faith to accept and believe in it.

To show the place of grace in human salvation, Paul gives us the controversial only-by-faith, only-by-grace (*sola fide, sola gratia*) passage: "For by grace you have been saved through faith, and this is not your own doing, it is the gift of God; it is not from works so that no one may boast" (Eph. 2:8-9). This is a clear statement that we are saved by grace, by what Jesus has done by his death on the cross. This is also a clear statement that our works do not count in the salvation of believers; only faith does. Furthermore, it is a declaration that we are saved through faith.

It is through faith that we respond to the work of grace by Jesus. This faith is what leads us to righteousness. When we accept what has been done to save us by faith, we are made right with God. This is why, using an interpretation of salvation history, Paul says that the Galatians should rely on faith in the Gospel he preached to them as the means to righteousness. For him, righteousness does not come by keeping the law or works of the law. Instead, it comes from faith, as can be seen from the Letter to the Hebrews: "The one who is righteous by faith will live" (2:4). Because Abraham's faith led to righteousness (Gen. 15:6), Paul concludes that those who have faith are children of Abraham and share in his blessings. This calls for some explanation. It is a disservice to interpret "faith alone" without reference to the other letters of Paul. This brought a major split in the Church and continues to divide believers in Christ. One reason for the split of Protestantism from Catholicism is Martin Luther's interpretation of Romans 3:28, "For we hold that a person is justified by faith apart from works prescribed by the law." Luther understood this as meaning that we are saved by "faith alone." Luther was so convinced of the importance of this viewpoint that he included the word "alone" in his translation of Romans 3:28, even though it is not in the original Greek text.

GRACE AND WORKS

The general concession is that grace is about the works of Jesus Christ, no more, no less. In other words, grace, God's work saves; human works do not save.

However, there are also works done in cooperation with grace that help to appropriate grace. Regarding these other works, Paul says, "For we are his workmanship, created in Christ Jesus for good works, which God prepared beforehand to be our way of life" (Eph. 2:10). If we are created in Christ Jesus for good works, and if good works should be our way of life, how then are works useless for salvation? This brings us to the different kinds of work taught by Paul.

It is important to note that the letters of Paul use "works" in two different ways. The first, "works of the law" (erga nomou), are mentioned in his letters to Romans and Galatians. The two letters are believed to be written by Paul himself in his lifetime. The second, "good works" (erga agatha), is mentioned only in his letter to the Ephesians, which is believed to be written by Paul's disciple after Paul's death. Here we see a new teacher who highlights new aspects of what Paul does not say in his other letters.

The two kinds of works are not the same. One refers to works of the law, which are ritual actions prescribed by the law for the Jews to fulfill for right living. In the Old Testament, it may be fulfilled by observing some ritual ordinances like circumcision, baptism, keeping the Passover feast, avoiding to each certain meats like pork, or washing of hands before eating (Lk. 11:38). The fulfillment of these rituals would make one righteous and a true Jew. However, these actions, in themselves, might not be morally good or bad but done because the law stipulates them to be done.

The other kind of works Paul calls good works refers to works and services done in cooperation with the grace of God. Jesus talks about it when he says: "In the same way, let your light shine before others, so that they may see your good works and give glory to your Father in heaven" (Matt. 5:16). These are the works James talks about when he says that "faith by itself if it has no works, is dead" (Jm. 2:17). The emphasis is on good works motivated by faith and aided by grace.

By James' standard, good works are important for salvation. Mathew tells us that the Last Judgment will be based on good works: "Then the king will say to those at his right hand, 'Come, you that are blessed by my Father, inherit the kingdom prepared for you from the foundation of the world; for I was hungry and you gave me food, I was thirsty and you gave me something to drink, I was a stranger and you welcomed me, I was naked and you gave me clothing, I was sick and you took care of me, I was in prison and you visited me. Truly I tell you, just as you did it to one of the least of these who are members of my family, you did it to me'" (Matt. 25:34-36, 40). It is not by our charity in itself that we are saved but charity done in response to the charity of Jesus and his teaching on charity or motivated by his self-giving sacrifice on the cross.

Good works are the result of good witness of life. It is the fruit of the Holy Spirit. It is the product of repentant life, and life surrendered to Christ. It is the effect of our cooperation with the work of grace of the Lord. It is the believers' response to the demands and teachings of Christ. It is what every Christian is called to do. It is a measure of faith and practice in the Lord. As a matter of fact, grace enabled works are the operating presence of Christ's salvation in our lives. It is God working in our lives through the power of his words, that enable us to break free from our sinful nature. This means that we need to cooperate with the transforming power of the word. Grace is one but we can have more of it when we dispose ourselves to receive it. We can have more of it by way of growth in works of faith.

So, we are saved by grace through faith unto good works. All three go together. All we need now is to accept and believe in the Lord's work of salvation for us, have faith in our belief, and measure how we cooperate with his grace by our good works. Faith shows itself by good works (Matt. 5:16). This goes to confirm that Christianity is not a religion of works but grace. As a religion of grace, we are saved and sustained by what Jesus has accomplished. We owe our salvation to him and his grace. All we need do is cooperate with his grace. Our good works are important to the extent that they are done in response to and cooperating with what God has accomplished through Jesus Christ for our salvation.

What therefore Paul is trying to say in his letters is that we are not saved by what we do or our human righteousness. Human righteousness is thought of as what we achieve through our works. When doing good works or observing the law is seen as a reward-oriented service, we see righteousness as what we earn or the fruit of our labor. When thus understood as the fruit of our labor, it leads to a sense of reward and entitlement. It is common in our society today to fall into the sense that we have a right to goods, natural resources, and education because of the taxes we pay. In this way, we develop the attitude that if we work hard, everything can be ours.

We are entitled to them. We begin to think that we have a right to something because of the role we have played. When we feel we have a right to things, we lose a sense of gratitude and stop recognizing that all we have is a gift from our good God. "What do you have that you did not receive? If then you received it, why do you boast as if it were not a gift?" (1 Cor. 4:7).

Sometimes we take this same attitude into the spiritual life. God must reward me if I say the right number of prayers, if I fast, if I obey this rule or that regulation. This Christian way of looking at reality is what Christ alluded to when he said to his disciples, "When you have done everything you were told to do, say, 'We are unworthy servants; we have only done our duty'" (Lk. 17:10). Here, Luke turns this attitude upside down. Jesus reminds us that we are always servants; everything comes to us as a gift. We are called to live in gratitude because all is given. Even our ability to work and to serve others is God's gift. These good works do not take the place of grace and cannot save in themselves. They are necessary for salvation as long as they are performed as a response to the work of salvation, as cooperating with the grace of God, or as enabled by grace.

So, a good understanding of Paul's letters will lead a sincere seeker to underscore that we are saved by grace. Our coming to faith in Christ is made possible only by God's grace. Our belonging to Christ is made possible only by faith in what he has done to save us. But our life as people who already believe in Christ is to be marked by good works. As God's militant saints, good works should be our way of life. What Paul condemns as irrelevant to justification or eventual salvation are works of the law, not good works. In this way, we see that God, who justified us by faith alone, does not save us by faith alone. The justified person must bear fruit of good works, fruit befitting repentance or risk of damnation on the judgment day (Matt. 7:16-23; Jn. 15:1-2).

CONCLUSION

Grace is the very character of God. It is a God-given desire and power to the Christian believer to do God's will. It takes grace on our part to respond to a relationship with God. By our nature, we choose ourselves and are selfish. It is God who takes the initiative to choose us (Jn. 15:16) draws us to himself (Jn. 6:44), and elevates us above our natural limitations to experience supernatural fellowship with him. This merciful condescension of divine love towards our created weakness is *grace*. Grace is the face that love wears when it meets imperfection or weakness or sin. Through grace, God meets us where we are, even when we sin. Then the ability to rise and not be dictated to by our fallen nature is grace. The Christian life is one saved and lived by grace through faith. By his death, he left us with the grace that enlightens us to see reality through the lens of God's eyes, think according to the mind of God, and act with a heart reminiscent of God's love.

As it were, there is no Christian life without grace, as there is no Christianity without grace. Hence the Christian life is the life of grace. Grace tells us that salvation is not what we do; it is what God has done and continues to do. Our upliftment and accomplishments are not what we do but what God uses us to accomplish. In other words, "not to us, not to us, but to God be the glory" (Ps. 115:1). We owe everything to him. To be true to the Christian faith is to realize and live by the fact that it is all by his grace.

If we knew the gift of God, if we could but realize when we experienced it, we would know that every time we come in contact with God something happens because in God is overflowing grace. This is so because our lives are surrounded by grace, even when we do not feel or notice it or when obscured by circumstances. There are moments we see God's face at work where he loves us. There is always a place and time when God is vivifying us, but it may not be spectacular. When what God promised us motivates us to serve others, or how we relate to others, or do good works, it is grace. Like the image of the mustard tree in the parable, Christ's grace sustains many men and women throughout the world. The Gospel seed carries an interior dynamism that affects souls and brings about change in them. Like the seed of the Gospel, it can grow silently without us knowing how.

So, grace is everything for the Christian. It divinizes us so that we share God's nature and marks us out for salvation. It is a participation in God's life. It is what makes life Christian after baptism. Hence to be a Christian is to live a life of grace. We can never have enough of it. As such, we can never stop growing in grace.

Now faith is the assurance of
things hoped for, the conviction
of things not seen.

And without faith it is impossible
to please him, for whoever
would draw near to God must
believe that he exists and that he
rewards those who seek him.

Hebrews 11:1,6

CHAPTER 3

IT IS A LIFE OF
Faith

The Christian life begins with faith in a God who created man, the earth, and heaven. This faith gradually forms and informs the believers' life and perspectives. Unfortunately, today, we live in a world of technology and science that tries to deny the existence of God. As a result, we are gradually being compelled to adopt a value system that in its quest for inclusivity, diminishes the ethics that point us to the higher Being. As things progress now in our world, it is not so much a case of people opposing God, but people who have come to a place where they believe that God is not needed. This not only makes the existence of God difficult to believe but also makes difficult our faith in God.

However, life, by its nature, is lived in and through faith. This is so because faith refers to a confident belief or trust in the truth about a person, an idea, or a thing. It is the persuasion of the mind that a certain thing or person is true. To have faith is to believe and trust in someone or something. Faith is not something vague or uncertain as some people think. It is a response of trust and belief in what is reliable, truthful, certain, and real. If I ask you now to stand up, and you did, and ask you again to sit, and you did, you will discover that you did not look behind to make sure your seat was there before you sat down. You would presume it is where it was before you stood up. It would be a presumption made in faith. In other words, you had faith that your seat was still where you had left it.

In this way, we see faith as a way of life. Everybody has faith in one thing or the other, which he allows to motivate his speech and give certainty to his action. It is faith in my mother that makes me eat my mother's food without any fear that there may be poison in it. I board a taxi without finding out whether the driver has a driver's license or not because I trust that he will drive me safely to my destination. I board and fly on an airplane once or twice a year without knowing the pilot's credentials but trusting it will be safe. I do all this with confidence because I trust the outcome will be good. I have faith in the pilots.

Faith is not only exercised with what is seen; it may also be an assurance about abstract things. For instance, we believe in the power of electricity even though we can't visibly see it with our naked eyes. We know we can tap into that power and use it to do things we could not do by our own human power. In this way, we say that faith is natural to the human person. In fact, it takes faith to believe in tomorrow, in my ability, and in my relationship with people. It takes faith to believe that when I sleep, I will not die in my sleep but will wake up in the morning. It is the engine with which human life is driven. One can say that without faith life has no meaning.

Faith in God works in a similar way. It is trust in God as a higher Being whose influence orders things right in their perspectives. The difference is that while faith can be exercised in everything according to their degrees of influence on the adherents, faith in God is a personal adherence to God. Though we do not see God, one of the greatest truths of God's revelation and our Christian faith is that we can know the one true and living God. *By his revelation*, "the invisible God, from the fullness of his love, addresses men and women as his friends, and moves among them, in order to invite and receive them into his own company. The adequate response to this invitation is faith" (CCC. 142).

Primarily speaking, faith is a gift of God. At the same time, it is a profoundly free and human act. The *Catechism of the Catholic Church* states it clearly: "Believing is possible only by grace and the interior helps of the Holy Spirit. But it is no less true that believing is an authentically human act. Trusting in God and cleaving to the truths he has revealed is contrary neither to human freedom nor to human reason" (CCC. 154). So, faith is not simply a matter of man's intellectual assent to truths about God but also human assent. We believe it when other people tell us about themselves and their intentions. We believe in and trust human promises. Similarly, it is common for our dignity to yield our intellect and will to God by faith and share in an interior communion with him (CCC. 154). In this way, faith is the divinely inspired human response to God's historical revelation through Jesus Christ.

In our own context as believers, faith is a gift of the Holy Spirit given to us in the sacrament of baptism that enables us to accept as true and life-giving all that God has revealed and taught us in and through the Church. There are three ways we can understand faith:

Faith understood as intellectual assent to doctrinal statements.

Faith understood as a total commitment and surrender of one's life to God.

Faith understood as allegiance to rules of life and ceremonies.

Faith, understood as intellectual assent to doctrinal statements, points to the faith that comes from listening and knowing the whole truth which God reveals to us through his word. The word of God, by its nature, has the ability to provoke faith. Preaching and teaching catechism aim to elicit faith in the hearer. In the doctrinal statements of the Church from the Bible and Tradition, God has revealed to us about himself, about ourselves, and about everything around us. It thus happens that, while God reveals himself and lets himself be known, a man comes to know who God is and, in knowing him, discovers himself, his origin, his destiny, the greatness, and the dignity of human life.

This knowledge one has about God provokes a response. The human response to it is faith. The more knowledge we have of God, the more faith we exercise. We can say that the size of our faith is equal to the size of our intellectual knowledge of God because the measure of the strength of a man's faith is ultimately the measure of his knowledge of God.

When our response turns into an act of faith, what we have come to know and accept about God begins to form and inform our vision of reality. This act of accepting revealed truth broadens the horizon of our knowledge and draws us to the mystery of the divine. So, while belief begins with knowledge, that is, with hearing about God and accepting the message, faith begins when we allow this knowledge and belief to model how we think and act.

As each of us grows in faith, these acts of faith "become an almost spontaneous habit" of inviting God into every situation.

Faith, understood as a person's adherence to God, is about trusting God and entrusting one's life to his grace. It is adhering oneself to God because of who he is and for the sake of what one has come to know about God. This faith response leads to a total commitment and surrender of self to God. This is achieved when what one knows and accepts about God and his teachings leads to a fruitful and confident surrender to the divine will. It is the faith expressed by Shadrach, Meshach, and Abednego when Nebuchadnezzar threatened to kill them if they refused to worship his God; "Even if our God will not save us, we want you to know, Your Majesty, that we will not serve your gods or worship the image of gold you have set up" (Dan. 3:18). In other words, they have committed themselves to God and will not change even if it means their death.

So, the faith here is adherence that comes from believing in the truth of the word of God. These words of Jesus, though, do not promise any rewards but have made martyrs and bequeathed faith. "What I tell you in the dark, say in the light, and what you hear whispered, proclaim on the housetops. And do not fear those who kill the body but cannot kill the soul. Rather fear him who can destroy both soul and body in hell" (Matt. 10:27-28). This calls for a fearless faith which shows itself in complete adherence of a person's entire being to trust God, a faith that is ready to take risks for the sake of God. It is the faith that made Mary accept God's proposal and says: "Behold, I am the handmaid of the Lord; let it be done to me according to your word" (Lk. 1:38).

This faith also refers to an uncompromising adherence to the tenets of one's religion. We see this faith in the uncompromising trust and personal commitment of Peter and Paul to Jesus.

Once, Peter responded to the hard teaching of Jesus about His body and blood thus: "Lord, to whom shall we go, you have the message of eternal life" (Jn. 6:68). In one of his letters, Paul expressed similar commitment thus: "I have been crucified with Christ; it is no longer I who live, but Christ who lives in me; and the life I now live in the flesh I live by faith in the Son of God, who loved me and gave himself for me" (Gal. 2:20). In these verses we see a faith-response which comes from their single-minded dedication to God and trust in Christ. This is the kind of trust that comes from personalizing the faith one professes or from receiving Jesus as the Lord of one's life.

Faith understood in this form comes from unbiased trust in God's faithfulness and ceaseless mercies (Lam. 3:22-23), from his protection and providence (Is. 41:10), or his everlasting love and forgiveness (Ex. 34:6). The faith response of this kind may be motivated by the greatness of God, fear of God, the awesomeness of God, divine providence, or divine promises. The believer exercising this faith, like Peter (Jn. 6:55), may not understand the theology of the Body and Blood of Christ referenced above but believes and stays with Jesus in a total commitment and surrender of one's life to God. For such believers, the difficulty they experience with a particular teaching of Jesus is not enough ground to give up following him. They go beyond believing by developing a personal love for the person of Jesus, which makes it possible to see him as the holy one of God who has eternal life. In this way, believing means surrendering oneself to God and entrusting one's destiny to him. It means entering a personal relationship with God and making this relationship the basis of one's entire life.

Faith, understood as allegiance to systems and rules of religion, describes human resolve to pledge allegiance to the principles and commandments governing one's religion. When we accept God as a fact of our lives and universe, we give allegiance to him with our whole hearts and souls. We also pledge our allegiance to his words and commandments.

Our allegiance to God and his commandments is an act of faith. It reflects a faith that views the Lord as Absolute and enthrones him as the universal King, the Lord of heaven and earth. If that is the case, *faith* in the Lord is best described as allegiance to him as King who deserves allegiance and whom we accept has the right of God to rule and reign over us by his commandments.

This faith is challenged and tested by both moments of scarcity and plenty. Yes, such moments challenge the exuberance of those of us who make promises when the journey is fresh but fail when the going becomes difficult. I have seen this among newlyweds and newly baptized adults. Some respond to the tenets of the faith with great zeal but decrease with time. We see it in some seminarians who enter the seminary with a deep sense of innocence and commitment but lose the fire of purity when they become senior seminarians. We see it among priests who are not only saintly but very dedicated when they are newly ordained but lose grip of their allegiance, dedication, spirituality, and holiness to pursue money or power later in their ministry. We see it among the newly professed Nuns who enter the Convent with a deep sense of morality and purity after the manner of the Blessed Virgin Mary, but with the passage of time, lose the fire of faith and purity and take to a new way of thinking and living that is opposed to that of our Lady who says: "I am the handmaid of the Lord, let it be done to me according to your word" (Lk. 1:38). It is these and similar situations that make Jesus pray for our stability to remain connected to him in truth and consecration (Jn. 17).

So, faith is tested by time and circumstances. As such, it is not enough to love and be loved, to believe and be baptized, but to remain faithful, dedicated, and loving in the face of temptations and life's challenges. Life is truly full of challenges, but they never overcome the man and woman of faith. Jesus tells us that our faith will withstand the storms of life if it is built on a firm foundation, one that consists of hearing the word of God and acting on it (Matt. 7:21-29). The Church wants Christians to be faithful in following the Lord at a young age and old age, in season and out of season.

Though faith can be understood in these three ways: intellectual assent to doctrinal statements, or adherence and total surrender of one's life to God, and surrender of one's life to God and as allegiance to systems and rules of religion, faith is one, and God is the reason for faith. As such, faith in all its ramifications is motivated by the power of who God is and what God does. Faith is not just a belief in the existence of God, as some people think. It is not what Paul calls "having a form of godliness but denying its power" (2 Tim. 3:5).

Some of these people in the Church recount the Creed every Sunday but live a godless life. Instead, faith looks at the power and action of God. It believes that God is able to do anything (Heb. 11:6) to deliver those who trust in him (Dan. 3:17). The word "to be able" means essentially "to have power" (*dunamai*, the verb form of the Greek noun, *dunamis*). God is able to save us completely (1 Pt. 1:15); He is able to keep us from sin (Heb. 2:18); He is able to supply our needs (2 Cor. 9:8); He is able to heal our diseases (Matt. 9:27-28); and He is able to deliver us from death (Dan. 3:17; 6:20; Heb. 5:7; Mk. 14:36). It is in our awareness and trust of God's power that we show we have faith in our belief in God.

Faith trusts God's power to create, protect, provide, and save. It trusts that God is Omnipotent and possesses infinite, complete, and perfect power. He can do absolutely anything because he holds all things in his power. The trust in God's power and saving ability enables the believer to take risks or wait on the Lord despite circumstances. He is a strong and mighty Lord (Ps. 24:8). Power belongs to him (Ps. 62:11). These divine attributes motivate and compel us to give assent, adherence, and surrender in trust to God.

THE CONTENT OF FAITH

Our Catechism teaches us that what moves us to believe is not the fact that revealed truths appear as true and intelligible in the light of our natural reason but the authority of God who reveals them. Thus, the miracles of Christ and the saints, prophecies, the Church's growth and holiness, and her fruitfulness and stability are motives of credibility that show that the assent of faith is "by no means a blind impulse of the mind" (CCC. 156). This is evident in Mark: "And they went forth and preached everywhere, while the Lord worked with them and confirmed the message by the signs that attended it" (Mk. 16:20). In this Mark's text, the Apostles' belief in the Lord illuminated their minds, convincing them of the truth, disposing them to testify it, and convicting the hearers of sin, righteousness, and judgment. The Lord was with them, confirming the truth of the Gospel with signs. In this, we see faith as a response of trust and belief in what is reliable, truthful, certain, and real.

As it were, we can know faith by its content because the act of believing has an object.

We cannot believe in a vacuum. We believe in someone or something of whom or of which we can give a description or call a name. God is the supreme object of faith. God is wise, powerful, and good. He is eternal and created the whole world out of nothing. He is one but three persons,

Father, Son, and Holy Spirit. In the person of Jesus, he became man for our salvation, and in the Holy Spirit lives in us.

Jesus, as God made man, is the visible content of faith. Every other divine gift or human acceptance is only a reflection of what God intended to accomplish and did accomplish in Christ. This is confirmed by the Letter to the Hebrews (Heb. 2:4), which tells us how preaching and deeds in the name of the Lord are accompanied by signs and wonders (Heb. 2:4). The grace of faith opens "the eyes of our hearts" (Eph. 1:18) to a lively understanding of the contents of the totality of God's plan and the mysteries of faith, and of their connection with each other and with Christ.

Jesus is the center of the revealed mystery. He provides us the content through his life, work, sacrificial death and resurrection, and God's promises. Jesus Christ is the true image of God and a reflection of his love. He came to give life and gave his life to save humanity. In him is the fulfillment of the promises of God, the Father, and the fulfillment of the law and the prophets (Matt. 5:17). Is it any wonder why he said to his disciples, "You have faith in God, have faith also in me" (Jn. 14:1).

Our knowledge of God is not simply limited to knowing some things about God and his nature, but we can know God personally through his Son, Jesus Christ. Jesus makes it possible for us to have a direct personal relationship and experiential knowledge of God as our loving and gracious Father. This is why to have seen Jesus is to have seen the Father (Jn. 14:9).

Because Jesus is the revelation of God, when we fall in love with him, we can know God through him. For this reason, the New Testament can describe Christ as the "author and finisher of our faith" (Heb. 12:1). All faith comes from and tends to him.

So, faith does not just exist. It is proactive and shows itself through divergent acts. As invisible as faith can seem to be, it reveals itself through personal works (Jm. 2:14). It can show itself through acts of charity or by an active submission to God and a willingness to do whatever he commands. It is in thinking about others and doing something for them that our faith in God increases and our relationship with him deepens. We can believe in God because he draws near to us and touches us through his son Jesus Christ. In fact, through the gift of faith, the Lord reveals himself to those who believe in his word.

In this way, faith is not abstract because it is about something concrete and substantial. As such, the world does not have a shortage of faith but a critical shortage of those who obey their faith. Even Jesus told his disciples that it is not their faith that is lacking when they asked him to increase their faith (Lk. 17:5). By their request, they seem to understand faith as something that can be quantitatively regulated by simply adding or subtracting. But Jesus said to them: "If you had faith like a grain of mustard seed, you could say to this mulberry tree, 'Be uprooted and planted in the sea,' and it would obey you" (Lk. 17:6). In this parable, Jesus implies that it is not their faith that is lacking. What is lacking is action. With this, Jesus makes the connection between faith and good works.

So, the disciples need to know that they still have enough faith to meet the demands of their discipleship. The real issue is not that the disciples need more faith; they need to exercise the faith they have, recognizing that it is a gift from God. Everyone has faith but not everyone exercises faith effectively. It is like these common sayings: It's not medicine until you take it. It's not a parachute unless you open it. It's not a song till you sing it. It's not *faith* until you *practice* it. James knew this, and he said:

"For just as the body without the spirit is dead, so faith without works is also dead" (2:26).

Faith needs action to bloom and blossom. When action is exercised, it puts faith into practice. This is why Jesus wants his disciples to exercise their faith always, no matter how little it may be, even when our prayers are not heard. He wants us to have faith in him, even and especially in moments of crisis, so we can triumph over them. This is the whole point Jesus wants his disciples to understand in the parable of the mustard seed (Matt. 13:31-32). He uses the parable to make his disciples understand that their little faith is still enough to meet the demands of discipleship. The real issue is not that the disciples need more faith; they need to put what they have to work. In other words, even faith the size of a mustard seed can do great things. Instead of feeling helpless in the presence of the great problems of our day, we can resort to the message which says, "Do what you can; it will be enough." God's grace will provide where human effort is inadequate. It is in exercising our faith in God that the child of God lives by faith.

FAITH AND THE WILL OF GOD

Faithfulness demands consistency and a determination to stay the course and see the task to its completion. This means that to have faith is one thing, and to endure in faith is another thing. It is easy to say that we have faith in the Lord when everything is going fine, but when problems arise, we show we have little or no faith to fall back upon. It is common that when we exercise faith, we expect God to respond right away. The truth is that as humans our life is lived by faith but willed by God.

Faith is not a magic wand but depends on God's will for a response. Though faith provokes a divine response to our prayers, it would be wrong to say that one will receive healing, for instance, every time one exercises faith. As a matter of fact, there are times we exercise faith, but for no fault of ours, no healing comes. Though healing may not come, our faith is still relevant. This is so because the faith required of us is not only the faith to believe that God is able to heal but also the faith to accept his will for us. While we will try to avoid or prevent suffering from happening and have faith that God can deliver us when they finally happen, we should also have faith to accept what our being in this world imposes on us and stop blaming God or becoming displeased with life. What it means is that we need faith that will remain even when things do not go our way or meet our expectations. In other words, we need faith strong enough to believe that God is able to deliver us (Heb. 11:6). It is God who executes the project, not us. All we need as believers in Christ is to trust and obey.

What this means is that faith is not measured by any other thing but by its object, Jesus, as can be seen in his love and works. Using the Gospel parable of the unprofitable servant (Lk. 17:7-10), Jesus teaches his disciples that faith does not look at life's difficulties but God's goodness. Yes, faith looks at God; it is interested in God only, talks about God and extols the virtues of God. To have faith in God means to hold on to the faithfulness of God.

This refers to God's faithfulness in his promises and their fulfillment. Anyone who holds on to the faithfulness of God does not seek their own interest but God's own interest.

THE NECESSITY OF FAITH

As invisible as faith seems, its place in life is invaluable. It is powerful, transformative, assuring, motivating, and audacious. Faith sees the invisible, believes in the incredible, and embraces the impossible. It offers hope in doubt, light in the darkness, and direction in confusion. It is not far-fetched why life, by its nature, is lived in and through faith. In a world where the future is unknown, the Christian needs trust to face it. Trust in what is real and in the One who is absolute and able is important to live a confident life. Trust is an invitation from our Lord during difficult times, financial difficulty, sickness, breakdown in relationship, bereavement, and the like. Trust does not magically remove these trials but guarantees that a person is not alone during such times. God is always present, pouring forth love, compassion, comfort, strength, and empowerment to the victim.

This means that faith has power. It has the power to make what is distant be felt concretely. What man cannot do with all his means can be achieved by the power of faith. Faith can pull out power from God of its own accord. We have some instances of this in the Scriptures. The woman with the issue of blood used her faith to pull out healing from Jesus (Lk. 8: 43-48); the ten lepers used faith to pull their restoration from the mouth of Christ (Lk. 17:19); the penitent prostitute used faith to receive salvation and forgiveness from Jesus (Lk. 7:50). So, with faith we touch the heart of Jesus and experience the power of his love. We open the door of grace with faith and receive God's approval. With faith, we move the mountain of fear, doubt, and adversity, and get over them. As such, an act of faith should accompany whatever the Christian does: be it planning, working, or conversing with people.

This is important because faith emits fire that spurs life into action. It is a spark plug that ignites the fire of conviction, tolerance, courage, and confidence. When the spark plug of faith is lit, and the grace of God is within us, whatever word we utter or prayer we say from the heart ignites through the Holy Spirit. It sets the Christian on fire for Jesus, a fire that neither time nor hardship can quench. The light of the spark plug of faith helps us see and interpret reality and life's challenges appropriately.

Is it any wonder why salvation is possible only by believing in Jesus Christ and in the One who sent him (Jn. 3:16; 6:40). As the Letter to the Hebrews puts it, "without faith it is impossible to please God" (11:6). Therefore, without faith, no one has ever attained justification, nor will anyone obtain eternal life. It is faith that assures us of eternal life even when we have not seen it and makes us taste in advance the light of the beatific vision, the goal of our journey here below. One then can say without mincing words that there is no salvation without faith.

So, it is not easy today and has never been easy to live without the light of faith. It takes faith to see a future during the dark hours of life. There are so many things happening that cause us to fear and doubt. All too often, we find ourselves in situations that are not what we planned: the denial of our God-given right to something, a sudden loss of job or a beloved person to death, or the experience of sudden illness. Each time we face a change in our plans, it takes faith to look beyond what appears like disappointment, to the grace God's plan has for us. The key to opening the door to the change of our vision is faith or trust. Thomas Merton says it well: "My Lord God, I have no idea where I am going. I do not see the road ahead of me. I cannot know for certain where it will end. Nor do I really know myself, and the fact that I think that I am following your will does not mean that I am actually doing so. But I believe that the desire to please you does in fact please you. And I hope I have that desire in all that I am doing. I hope that I will never do anything apart from that desire. And I know that if I do this you will lead me by the right road though I may know nothing about it. Therefore, will I trust you always though I may seem to be lost and in the shadow of death. I will not fear, for you are ever with me, and you will never leave me to face my perils alone." In other words, faith consists in believing when it is beyond the power of reason to believe. That is to say that at times faith takes us to that place beyond which reason fails.

We know people who say their faith carried them in their darkest hours. This is why the Christian life can never be lived without faith. Let us be clear: anger cannot help solve life's challenges. If we swear like Job and curse out the day we were born (Job 3), it will not stop our misery. If we cry like Jeremiah (20:14-15) and blame our misery on our parents or the circumstances of our birth, it will never add one cubit to our span of life (Matt. 6:27). Our problem can never be solved by negative responses but by faith and trust in God's providence, liberation, vindication, loving-kindness, mercy, and salvation. The point is that faith helps us to be positive in the face of our teething challenges and to pray to God and say, "Lord, help me to walk, not by sight but by faith. There is no doubt that we need faith today more than ever.

The good news is that faith is a ladder with which we climb the challenges of life. While faith is possible, it is not easy. Even though enlightened by Him in whom it believes, faith is often lived in darkness and can be put to the test. The world we live in often seems very far from the one promised to us by faith. Our experiences of evil, suffering, injustice, and death seem to contradict the Good News at times; they can shake our faith and become a temptation against it (CCC. 164).

It takes the witnesses of faith to avert this and turn to Abraham, who "in hope believed against hope" (Rom. 4:18), to the Blessed Virgin Mary, who, in "her pilgrimage of faith," walked into the "night of faith" (Lg. 58) in sharing the darkness of her son's suffering and death. With the ladder of faith, we climb over our fear, impediments, sickness, and misfortune and pull power out of Jesus of its own accord. In fact, we can never exhaust the necessity of faith. It is the hub on which the relationship with God is driven, devotion-motivated, and mission inspired. It helps us respond to life's daily challenges with our eyes fixed on God's promises.

CONCLUSION

As we can see, faith is the oil with which a relationship with God is driven. It is first and foremost a belief in One, Great and Almighty God as Lord and Father. It is a belief in his love for me which is manifest in how he sent his only begotten Son, Jesus Christ, to redeem me. It is a belief in the communion I have with him, which is made possible by the Holy Spirit he sent to the Church and to me. It is a belief that as a son or daughter, I am not only a creature but a redeemed child of God who lives for God in all things as an implication of who I am in God.

It is not an exaggeration to say that faith is what makes a Christian. It is indispensable for life and Christian living because Christians live by faith. This faith is more than mere assent to certain teachings and dogmas of the Church in the Bible or Tradition. It is much more than believing in the truths about God because it takes faith to have conviction in our belief. While every believer has faith, not every one of them has total commitment and surrender to God and his teachings. In this lies the faith that makes a believer authentic and true to the name. It is, first and foremost, the adherence of a person's entire being to God and his grace. Pope Benedict articulated this beautifully in his first encyclical: "Being Christian is not the result of an ethical choice or a lofty idea, but the encounter with a person or an event, which gives life a new horizon and a decisive direction" (Deus Caritas Est 1). It is from this encounter that one then believes that whatever God has revealed is true. There is first an encounter and second, trust in the God encountered. In other words, there is belief, then trust and transformation. So, when a person encounters Christ, his life goes from trust to obedience. This confirms that faith as an act of obedience is a means by which a person commits oneself to God.

To be a Christian then is to have an active and living faith. This makes us understand that faith is never a one-time event but a life-long process. It does not remain fixed after a single conversion experience. It can grow or be dwarfed. It can be shipwrecked (1 Tim. 1:19), misplaced (1 Tim. 6:21) or lost (Jm. 1:17). As such, every true Christian takes steps to develop his faith so that he can withstand the challenges of the godless society we find ourselves, in a society that is infested with the evils of injustice, fraud, wickedness, deceit, hatred, moral decadence, and war.

So, just as Rome was not built in a day, faith is not a once and for all achievement. It grows and increases. Every effort is to be made to develop our faith. Developing and growing is a task every true Christian undertakes with a concrete sense of commitment. This is important because faith, by its nature, is elastic; it endures, perseveres, and withstands odds and obstacles. Faith is *certain*. It is based on the very word of God, who cannot lie or change. He is the one who opens the eyes of the mind to assent to the truth and believe it. We are able to believe in God because he draws near to us and touches us. Through the gift of faith, the Lord reveals himself to those who believe in his word.

In line with this is the understanding that as powerful as our faith can be, it is not a measure of God's faithfulness and love for his people.

As the way of being Christian, faith enlightens the believer to know that God is much more than what he does. As a result, it is wrong to judge or measure him by what he does or does not do. A true Christian, then, is one who walks by faith, not by sight, and believes that the only way to enjoy life is through faith.

Therefore, as far as religion is concerned, faith is everything. It is not only the thing that makes religion active but also real and meaningful. Faith is the only way we can enjoy the Christian life. In fact, no faith, no Christianity. This is why a faithless Christian is not only a visionless person but a clueless and helpless Christian. "Therefore, since we are surrounded by so great a cloud of witnesses, let us also lay aside every weight and sin which clings so closely, and let us run with perseverance the race that is set before us, looking to Jesus the pioneer and perfecter of our faith." (Heb. 12:1-2).

> For I know the plans I have for you, plans to prosper you and not to harm you, plans to give you hope and a future.

Jeremiah 29:11

CHAPTER 4

IT IS A LIFE OF
Hope

We live in a world of so much hopelessness, despair, doubt, distrust, and depression. Nothing gives confidence and assurance of a better tomorrow. Our economy is fragile, and many are living in hunger and thirst. Relationships are entered into today and lost tomorrow. There is widespread hate and deceit, and wrongful convictions abound. It is not easy to pay one's way through the University for lack of funds, and even when we can, in the end, unemployment stares one in the face. Often things appear at a standstill, and there is nowhere to turn. These are the realities today for people all over the world. There is nothing worth trusting or risking one's life. It is not only a challenge to imagine any future in which things are constantly changing, but it is hard to think of a future in which things are somewhat positive. Things are so overwhelmingly bad. There is no optimism about the future. How can we have hope in such a world of hopeless situations?

WHAT IS HOPE?

The human person is a bundle of desires and dreams. We are always wishing things into existence. But in our consciousness, we realize that our desires differ from our situation. In reality, we find ourselves suffering and limited in our choices. In our daydreams, we achieve the proper object of our desires, but in our actual lives, we find ourselves grounded and roam about in one place. It then dawns on us that desires and dreams are but unreal. However, such knowledge does not mean an end. As such, there is no need to play the blame game in difficult situations when there is light to turn. One of the functions of hope is to help us at such a time lift our eyes to the light at the end of the tunnel. This confirms that hope takes much of its root in the innate impulses of one's soul. Even though our limitations bring us down, something deeper keeps directing our lives. A deeper part of us retains the memory of God's promises and assurances. Life's challenges may blur the memory but cannot erase God's plan and gift of a future of hope for believers. Hope is innate to the extent that despite life's challenges, we are convinced that we have individual significance and destiny. In this way, hope makes peace with the circumstances confronting our lives.

Hope for some can be a mere wish. "I hope I am given a pair of shoes this Christmas." "I hope that my brother passes his examination." "I hope that my mother recovers from her sickness." "I hope that scientists find a cure for coronavirus." But hope is much more than mere wishes. It combines the desire for something and the expectation of receiving it. It is an optimistic attitude of the mind based on an expectation or desire. In this case, it refers to the desires of the heart. "Take delight in the Lord, and he will give you the desires of your heart" (Ps. 37:4). "Give all your worries and cares to God, for he cares about you" (1 Pt. 5:7). "May these words of my mouth and this meditation of my heart be pleasing in your sight, Lord, my Rock and my Redeemer" (Ps. 19:14). All these quotations are about hope and call for faith to believe. They point to a hope that someday something will happen; a favor will come.

In this way, hope is the ability to face the odds of life with a sense that there is something we can do about them. It helps us create other behaviors that make things easier or fuel more hope. It helps to build resiliency to withstand difficult situations. In other words, having hope is having expectations that something good will happen in the future. It is about anticipating a positive outcome through perseverance and effort. Hope is looking forward to "something" with desire and patient endurance.

WHAT IS CHRISTIAN HOPE?

Hope is one of the theological virtues. Christian hope takes its root in our creeds, in what Christ revealed and did for us. It is the theological virtue by which we desire the kingdom of heaven and eternal life as our happiness, placing our trust in Christ's promises and relying not on our own strength but on the help of the grace of the Holy Spirit (CCC. 1817). Our Christian hope is the confident expectation of what God has promised, and its strength is in his faithfulness.

Though a theological virtue, hope is still different from faith. Some people mistakenly think that hope and faith can be used interchangeably. Faith and hope are distinct and related. They are complementary. While faith is grounded in the reality of the past, hope is looking to the reality of the future. While faith has a rational sense of certain expectations, hope has an emotional sense of expectation. For instance, when Herod saw

Jesus, he was exceedingly glad; for he had desired for a long time to see him because he had heard many things about him and hoped to see some miracle done by him (Lk. 23:8). Faith is trust in a person or thing or a belief not based on proof, while hope is an optimistic attitude of mind based on desire or expectation. Faith comes before hope. If faith is the substance of what is hoped for, it takes faith to set one's hope on something, to believe that what we hope for will be realized. This is so because faith agrees with reality, and hope is congruent with dreams.

Faith tells us there is a Father, God, who does miracles. He can heal the sick and raise the dead. Trust him. Hope tells us that God will do a miracle for us. It will happen sometime, someday. He has the plan to give you a future of goodness and favor (Jer. 29:11). Expect it; hope in him. Faith says that God exists, and hope says we are not alone; God is with us. We are not alone in our daily struggles. Though our world may be scary and sometimes evil, God promised he would not leave us alone. As those baptized in the name of the Father, the Son, and the Holy Spirit, we live in Christ, who also lives in us, the hope for glory (Col. 1:27).

Therefore, hope is not in what we can see but in what we cannot see. The hope that is seen is not hope, for who hopes for what he already sees? But if we hope for what we do not see, with perseverance, we wait eagerly for it (Rom. 8:24,25). It is like a man who sows seed on his farm and fears it might not mean anything. However, he somehow believes it will grow significantly into a great iroko tree, although the scorching of the wind and sun it must experience to become a tree it cannot even see. Following this, hope waits for a good outcome despite challenges. It knows that life is full of struggles and puts on resiliency and endurance. This can be demonstrated with a story about two frogs. Two frogs fell into a deep cream bowl. One was wise and a cheery soul. The other one took a gloomy view and bade his friend a sad adieu. The other frog with a merry grin said: "I can't get out, but I won't give in; I'll swim around till my strength is spent. Then I will die the more content." And as he swam, though ever it seemed, his struggling began to churn the cream. Until on top of pure butter, he stopped. And out of the bowl, he quickly hopped. The hope that the struggle will have a happy ending made the frog with a merry grin, endure the hurdle. In the case of human beings, it is not just the thought that things might get better - but that no matter what happens, a person knows that God loves him - and that God accompanies him.

THE BASIS OF HOPE

In the Old Testament, hope is rooted in the character of God, past deeds of salvation, and covenant with Israel. The covenant assures the people of God's care, love, and salvation. He is a faithful God for them, and his promises can never fail. Even in the darkness of their exiles, they believed God would come to their rescue. This is so because love is God's nature, and his steadfast love is never doubted. As the book of Lamentations says, "The love of God does not cease, and his mercies do not come to an end. They are new every morning" (Lev. 3:22-23). It is on account of this that the author of Lamentations further says, "'The Lord is my portion,' says my soul, 'this I call to mind, therefore I will hope in him'" (Lam. 3:24). He holds on to the certainty of God's love and faithfulness that even amidst the misery and discouragement that dominate Lamentations, there is room for hope. It was then their knowledge of God's faithfulness to the covenant, the way he led them out of Egypt that gave them enough reasons to trust in God's capacity to do again what he had performed in the past.

As a result, the people of the Old Testament had the courage to hope for big things: that the desert would be turned into fertile land, that their scattered and divided people would eventually be gathered again, that the blind would see, the deaf hear, and the lame walk. They also hoped that their people and all the peoples of the earth would be united in the blessings of everlasting peace (Is. 35:1-5).

On the other hand, Christian hope is founded on the promises of Jesus, his trustworthiness, and the evidence of his resurrection. In this way, Christian hope then is based on what has happened and not on wishful thinking. It is that which has happened that provokes hope for that which eyes have not seen. "And hope does not disappoint us, because God's love has been poured into our hearts through the Holy Spirit who has been given to us" (Rom. 5:5). In this passage, Paul sees suffering as something worthwhile, a growing certainty that our ultimate destiny is an eternity of good in God's presence. He then concludes that this hope can never put us to shame. In other words, our hope will be fully vindicated. We will never, in the end, be disappointed in hoping to receive God's goodness forever. If God gives us the Holy Spirit, there is nothing he cannot give us. As a result, Christians are confident about their ultimate destination because God's love has been poured into our hearts. It is a way of saying that God will keep his promises because he loves us. It is not because God is able to do what he has promised or because he is good. It is because God cares about us and loves us to the extent that each one of us carries his love inside through the Holy Spirit. This inward experience of God's love produces hope.

How is the resurrection of Christ another source of hope? It is true that death is a threat, and some people live in perpetual fear of it. While some cannot stand the mention of death, others are ready to develop high blood pressure if they discuss it. All this is because we see death as an end. Against this background, Jesus demonstrated by his death and resurrection that there is life after death. In so doing, he causes believers to hope in life after death. With this, Jesus tells us that death is not the end of life but a transition from this life to eternal life. As a matter of fact, life would be meaningless if there were no resurrection, and God cannot make that mistake and still be the God of the living and the dead.

On Good Friday hope died, but after three days, Jesus resurrected from the dead and restored hope. Jesus, the resurrected, now lives forever with the Father and us. Because he lives with Father, our hopes are not broken but fulfilled. Our future is not destroyed but perfected. Our life is not in danger but secured for all eternity. This way, we live in the hope that is not vague, in the hope that gives certainty and courage to face the future. This makes tolerable the sufferings of the present moment, which are not comparable to future glory (Rom. 8:18). By his resurrection, we have been born anew to a living hope (1 Pt. 1:3). Though at times we experience loneliness, Christians are not alone in their struggles. The Lord is on our side. Now this is hope; this is hope that never disappoints. We believe and celebrate that every encounter with him brings something great. As a result, we hope for lasting peace, true love for one another, peaceful lives, good political leadership, food sufficiency, and an end to wars and suffering, pain, and misery. In fact, we all hope for a better tomorrow.

So, believers in Christ hope for the same things as the Old Testament people but differ from them in two ways. First, the coming of Jesus in history, as partial fulfillment of God's promises, confirms and strengthens our hope. The fact that God promised and fulfilled what he promised at the appointed time gives us hope to believe that he would fulfill other promises that are not yet realized. Secondly, we differ from the Old Testament people because Jesus revealed that God is not far off but is already in our midst. Because God is with us, we know we can encounter the touch of God's healing love and presence when we pray, read, and reflect on the Bible, in almsgiving and charity, in corporal works of mercy, in forgiving and being forgiven, giving and receiving gifts. Hope tells us that engaging in these activities brings rewards and opportunities to encounter the Lord.

In this way, the hope we are discussing is different from optimism. It is different from the conviction that something will turn out well. Rather, it is the certainty that something makes sense, regardless of how it turns out. So, hope is waiting but not aimless waiting. It is a celebration of the fact that God does come to those who stand and wait. It celebrates that those who wait for the Lord's coming encounter him in one form or another. We do not only believe that the Lord will come and always comes, but we also believe that his coming will bring something great. This is our undying hope. It is the hope that when he breaks in upon me, my sin will be forgiven and my guilt wiped out, my worries will disappear, and my fear will turn into faith; my test will turn into a testimony, and my sorrow will be overcome with joy, and my hatred will turn into love. Since these are all possible when I welcome his words, the hope of experiencing him helps me yield to his life-liberating and transforming words.

Hope has long been a way of Christian living. It sustained the early Christians when what they thought about the life and leadership of Jesus did not materialize. They found themselves in an apparently hopeless predicament soon after Jesus left them to the Father, and were massively oppressed and persecuted by the Jewish religious hierarchy. Their belief that the Second Coming of the Lord Jesus was soon to take place encouraged them to endure the persecution. They believed and hoped it would coincide with the fall of Jerusalem and the destruction of the Temple. But when in AD 70 Jerusalem fell and the Temple was destroyed, and yet Jesus was nowhere to be seen, the Christians found themselves in a big crisis of faith. It felt like they had hoped in vain. It felt like their enemies would now treat them with ridicule.

Should they continue to hope and resist the injustices of their oppressors, or should they join them since they cannot beat them?

However, despite the pressure, they did not give up but believed in a better tomorrow, like Abraham, who, "hoping against hope, believed" (Rom. 4:18). This does not make hope be seen as a play of "trial and error." It rather means that there are, in fact, certain things that happen, and the only way to cope is to hope against hope. We do so because hope is about a future we do not have here and now, a peaceful assurance that something that has not happened yet will indeed occur. It involves something unseen: "For in this hope we were saved. Now hope that is seen is not hope. For who hopes for what he sees?" (Rom. 8:24).

It is important to note that as it is in our human nature to lose hope when things do not go as planned, the response of the disciples to the death of Jesus was one of hopelessness. They thought it best to leave the city or hide from the authorities. They withdrew to themselves, and hope was gone. They went away, each to his former business. But in this darkest moment of their lives, Jesus showed up at the Sea of Tiberias to prove to them that his promise to be with them was worth believing and hoping for.

The indisputable message is that we can never stop hoping. At times, all we must do is hope against hope. Though there is so much darkness in life and in the world, we need the light of hope to let a shaft of light break through the heavy clouds. In other words, we cannot but hope even when there seems insufficient grounds to have a particular hope. This is the Christians' response to the darkness around us.

CONCLUSION

So, to live a Christian life, we need hope. Life is not easy, has never been easy, and will never be easy if it is lived on this earth. It takes hope to pull through the many challenges of life. When life's experiences present us with a difficult situation, we wage a campaign of passive resistance against them without knowing when they may come to an end. We do so very instinctively because hope is response oriented. What it means is that we need hope to work, love, relate and enjoy living. It is the message or story of our hope that inspires and empowers those who come in contact with us.

Adversities often challenge our life. It takes hope to cope and bounce back from setbacks. Hope gives us the strength and determination to keep going, even when things are difficult, by instilling the belief that things can improve, allowing us to navigate challenging times with greater resilience and perseverance. It assures us that God is present with us in our pain and offers comfort, strength, and assurance. In other words, hope fuels our motivation as believers to work towards our goals, overcome obstacles, and persist in facing challenges.

In counseling, hope is crucial in maintaining positive mental and emotional well-being. It provides counselees with a deep sense of optimism and helps combat feelings of despair, anxiety, and depression. Hope, in fact, offers a ray of light during dark times, lifting our spirits and enabling us to see possibilities beyond our current circumstances. In this way, it provides us with a sense of purpose and direction.

Christian hope is transformative. It inspires the Christian to pursue personal transformation and moral growth. It believes that through the power of the Holy Spirit, believers can experience inner renewal, overcome sin, and cultivate virtues such as love, forgiveness, compassion, honesty, courage, fidelity, integrity, and humility. In this way, hope motivates Christians to strive for holiness and become more Christ-like in character.

The sequel to transformation is that hope enables personal growth by encouraging us to explore new possibilities, set ambitious goals, and strive for self-improvement. It pushes us beyond our comfort zones, empowering us to take risks and embrace opportunities for growth. In fact, with hope, we can unlock our full potential and achieve things we once thought were impossible.

Hope is essential for meaningful Christian living because it is a powerful motivator, fosters resilience, supports mental and emotional well-being, strengthens relationships, and promotes personal growth and achievement. When we have hope, we believe our efforts can lead to better outcomes and a brighter future. In this way, hope gives us the courage to face tomorrow, embrace change, believe in possibilities, and be patient with ourselves and the things around us, even in the face of challenges and adversity. Hope then is positive and characterizes the living. While a person is alive, he cannot help but hope.

So, hope is characteristic of who we are as human beings. It belongs to our very nature.

"While there is life, there is hope, and more so for the Christian believer. Christian hope tells us that there is certainty despite the uncertain things of life and that there is light despite the presence of darkness (Eccles. 9:4). It provides comfort and assurance that, through faith in Christ, one can be reconciled with God, receive forgiveness of sins, and have the hope of spending eternity in his presence. It then brings solace and peace to the Christian in the face of mortality and the uncertainties of life. In this way, it inspires believers to live in accordance with their faith, seek justice, love and serve their neighbors, and find purpose in glorifying God and participating in his redemptive work in the world.

As a light in the darkness, hope is trustful. It does not see all that is involved in a matter but believes in positive outcomes despite circumstances. It chooses to stand on promises and not allow odds to becloud its vision. It does not relent in all that it does. It is always hopeful. Hope provokes action, a response. To live and not have hope is to live without real meaning in life. Hope helps us see purpose in life through Jesus Christ, whose life and resurrection have taught Christians how to face tomorrow without fear.

> Love is patient, love is kind.
> It does not envy, it does not
> boast, it is not proud. It does not
> dishonor others, it is not self-
> seeking, it is not easily angered,
> it keeps no record of wrongs.

1 Corinthians 13:4-5

CHAPTER 5

IT IS A LIFE LIVED IN
Love

ove is very central in Christianity and could be called the religion of love. This is so because God, the Creator, is love. He cannot but love because it is in his nature to love. The idea of creating humans in his own image has nothing to do with how we look but with our capacity to be loving and caring as God is and does. In fact, creation and all within it show the love of God. The human person is not only the apex of creation but also the one in whom love is most expressed. This makes God's relationship with the human person a unique one.

Introducing himself to Moses at a time Moses was afraid that the sins of the Israelites would not be forgiven, God said: "The Lord, the Lord, the compassionate and gracious God, slow to anger, abounding in steadfast love and faithfulness" (Ex. 34:6). With this God gives an idea of who he is and how he acts. He rules with love, and so connects all he created with love. "The Lord is good to all, and his compassion is over all that he has made" (Ps. 145:9). It is love that has no frontiers and knows no bounds but is universal. This is manifested by how God created the human person in his image. He leaves the mark of his love in every relationship with his people. In other words, love is of God and his nature and character.

In his love for the world living in sin, he gives Jesus his only begotten son to pay the price for sin to save the world (Jn. 3:16). He is freely offered as the atoning sacrifice for our sins and the sins of the world out of love for our well-being. His love is sacrificial; he does not count what it costs him to love, even when it means the death of his only Son, Jesus Christ. The love of God is certain and can be trusted. "I have loved you with an everlasting love, and I am constant in my affection for you" (Jer. 31:3). With this, he teaches humanity that love is at the center of relationships. It is the oil with which God's relationship with his children is driven.

This love of God is everlasting because nothing can stop God from loving us.

It is a faithful love that neither ceases nor comes to an end but is renewed each day even as we fail in our commitments (Lam. 3:22-23). It is a forgiving love because no matter what we do, God loves us despite our failures. Love makes God treat us not according to what we deserve but what we need. He sees our needs through the eyes of his love. He sees our need for a Savior and sends Jesus to save us with his love. He wants love to be the heart of our lives because his love is eternal.

JESUS IS THE REFLECTION OF THE LOVE OF GOD

The word of God teaches us that God is love (1 Jn. 4:16) and that Jesus is the love of God who came down from heaven (Jn. 3:16). He is the love of God made manifest. In other words, he is the incarnated love of God, the reflection of his loving heart and tender loving care. In Jesus, we see the love of God in practice. "God proves his own love for us, in that while we were yet sinners, Christ died for us" (Rom. 5:8).

The heavenly Father is a compassionate God. In Jesus, God's compassion is made manifest. Compassion is love prompted by the heart. It is love that identifies with the suffering person's grief and physical condition. Compassion means suffering with or feeling the pain and distress the other person feels. It is putting oneself into the position of the other and trying to see things the way the other person sees them. Jesus relates to people with a love that comes from the heart.

Compassion is Jesus' sense of love and motivation throughout his ministry. In several places, the Gospel records that Jesus was "moved to the depth of his heart" when he met with individuals and groups of people. During this time, Jesus did not only do something about the needs of the people but also felt their pain and distress. He expressed God's compassionate love by recognizing and identifying with outcasts, feeding the needy, giving care to the bereaved, giving health to the blind, dumb, deaf, and crippled, raising the dead, showing compassion to those unjustly treated and interacting with sinners and tax collectors (Mk. 2:13-17). Love and compassion motivated his preaching, his charity, and his miracles throughout his ministry.

Motivated by the same love, Jesus offered himself to be sacrificed for the salvation of the world. On the Cross, he demonstrated the height of his love for humanity. What motivated him to lay down his life on the Cross as the atoning sacrifice for the sin of the world is love for his Father in heaven and love for every one of us who are made in the image and likeness of God. This way of loving tells us that true love does not count the cost involved in the relationship. The cost involved in the message of the Cross of Christ that is, the self-giving of himself to be crucified for the people, is priceless. The means to this is very scary: he was hated, humiliated, falsely accused, crowned with thorns, and executed by hanging. These experiences are enough to dissuade him from loving to the point of death, especially when those he died for did not care about him. But, motivated by the goal he set out to accomplish, namely, the world's salvation, he accepted to damn the consequence.

The pain and suffering of Jesus are the sources of salvation because they came from his selfless love for humanity. As Jesus puts it himself, "Greater love has no one than this that one lay down his life for his friends" (Jn. 15:13). Jesus laid down his Godhead, status, personality, power, and joy in the name of love for the well-being of the people. This unselfish love is the high point of the passion of Christ.

So, on the Cross, God reveals the breadth of his great love for sinners and the power of redemption, which cancels the debt of sin and reverses the curse of our condemnation. Jesus gave his Father supreme honor and glory through his obedience and willingness to sacrifice his life on the Cross. In so doing, he teaches us that love motivates true obedience, not force. He once told his disciples this: "If you love me, keep my commandments" (Jn. 14:21). In other words, it takes love to obey God's commandments, not compulsion or pressure. It is a common saying that the greatest trust one can give to his commander is the willingness to obey in the line of duty, even to the point of putting oneself in harm's way. However, it will be seen as forced if it is not done with love as its motivation.

On the Cross, we see a new way of loving, a love that is unselfish and selflessly oriented to serving others for their good, and a generous love that is forgiving and merciful beyond comprehension. The example of this love in action is shown in the foot washing of the Apostles when Jesus becomes the servant of the disciples and washes their feet (Jn. 13:1-17). Jesus loves his disciples as equals, and that is what makes this commandment so new (Jn. 13:34). A master is seen as a superior to be worshiped with fear and trembling, but Jesus does not only stoop low to his disciples but also falls in love for them. This is the love that will mark believers in the world of superiority, hate, and division. With this, Jesus declares love as Christian Identity. Our future as disciples depends on our understanding of this new commandment and in putting it into practice. This radical way of loving one another will also become the visible sign by which all will know who we are as disciples of Jesus. "By this all men will know that you are my disciples, if you have love for one another" (Jn. 13:35).

As we can see, in Jesus Christ, God gives us an example of unconditional love. Jesus lived out this love, not because he wanted to please anyone or was forced, but because love is in his nature. He served us with it not because we deserved it but because we needed it. He looked beyond his own need to satisfy our own needs. He had every reason not to love this much and kept his peace. He was very young and would have loved to enjoy life more. He had many fans when he was on the earth and would have loved to enjoy their company more by living longer. But he considered the needs and well-being of the people much more than all this, and he gave his life out of love to save us. This is selfless love. There is no sincere way we can believe in what he did out of love, celebrate it, and not be affected and transformed by it. Hence love is the Christian heartbeat.

LOVE FOR THE NEIGHBOR

The love of God, which Jesus physically reflects, is universal. He does not keep it to himself but shares it with creation. God's love for each one of us is as real and tangible. It is like a love of a lover who gives all for his beloved. In fact, God made us in love for love. He made us to know him personally, grow in the knowledge of his great love for us, and to love him and humanity in return. He makes this possible by giving us a share in his love so we may love as he does. In Jesus Christ, we share in the love of God, the Father. Just as Jesus reflects God's love, we are baptized in Christ to reflect his love to the world.

Jesus, through whom God has given us his love, teaches his disciples and all of us the love of the Father and how to share it with one another. Jesus has given us an example of this love and made us share in it. Paul tells us that "God's love has been poured into our hearts through the Holy Spirit which has been given to us" (Rom. 5:5). So, we already have this selfless love of Christ in spite of our human view of love. We are carriers of God's divine love. This love God pours into us through the Holy Spirit is the one which fuels and motivates the love we share with others. As such, we have the capacity to love and share love from the reservoir of his divine love in us.

Jesus is an example of how love is shared. His love seeks the well-being of the other. He does not keep his love to himself; he reaches out and shares himself and his gifts with others. He reflects his love in how he teaches and interacts with his disciples. With them, he teaches that love is not lording over but sharing oneself with others. He loved his disciples as friends.

He addressed his disciples as friends to show this heavenly side of his love. "No longer do I call you servants, for the servant does not know what his master is doing; but I have called you friends, for all that I have heard from my Father I have made known to you" (Jn. 15:15). It is the culture of the Jews to call one who trains under a teacher a slave or servant. As men who did not make it to the rabbinical school and were called to follow Jesus, the apostles started their relationship with Jesus as servants, but Jesus transformed it into friendship. Jesus considers this change particularly important so that it will change the way disciples relate to him. Loving one another as equals will be the divine dynamic that will keep the presence of Jesus alive and active in our midst even after he has physically returned to the Father. This way, he shares his love with the disciples and the people; he teaches the disciples to do likewise with their love for one another.

As a matter of fact, love for the neighbor was a commandment well known to the people before Jesus came to the earth. The rabbis taught and recited it every Sabbath (Lev. 19:9-18). "You shall love your neighbor as yourself. I am the Lord" (Lev. 19:18). In exercising this law of love for others, the selfish interpretation of the rabbis takes it out of context. The love of the human person for self becomes the parameter to measure love for the other. During his ministry, Jesus revolutionized the command: "Love your neighbor as yourself" (Lev. 19:18) and replaced it with "Love your neighbor as I have loved you" (Jn. 13:34). While the command is still about the love of the neighbor, the motive behind it is different. Jesus' love is the paradigm to measure true love for others and not that of the human person, which is exercised as a person thinks or wants. True love is lacking in some people. For such persons, there would be a disaster if they were to love their neighbor as they love themselves. It is obvious that some persons are yet to be transformed to the unconditional love of the Father, exemplified in the ministry of Jesus and on the Cross for us. The selfless and sacrificial love of Jesus remains the reference point and parameter to measure love for others. To love this way is to see all things reconciled in the Lord and to regard people not according to human standards but by the standard of Christ.

The love for the other is selfless. It has the well-being of the other at heart. It is opposed to our human view of reality. It goes beyond sentimentality in a world where the true meaning of love is lost to selfish interest, compromise, or favoritism. Christian love becomes an ideal. Jesus bases his call to this universal love on God's behavior. God blesses the good and the bad alike. He makes his sun rise on the bad and the good and causes rain to fall on the just and the unjust. Jesus, after the manner of God, loves both good and bad people to the point of dying to save them. Love for the other is not discriminatory. It is universal and accommodative.

Because love creates a union, Jesus teaches his disciples and future disciples to make love the mark of their union. Love for the other is Jesus' last will and the distinguishing mark by which "all will know that you are my disciples" (Jn. 13:35). Jesus does not just love us with the love of God but wants us, as his disciples, to love as he has loved us (Jn. 13:34; 15:13). He does not only call us as disciples to preach but also to share the love. We will be known by our commitment to love. This is what it means to be a Christian, to love others with the boundless love of Jesus our Lord.

THE CHALLENGES OF IMPLEMENTING THE LOVE FOR THE OTHER

Our God is love. He not only loves himself and his people but also commands his people to love one another. "You shall love your neighbor as yourself" (Lev. 19:18). In the exercise of this commandment, the chosen people discriminated against those who were not their "neighbors ."This is so because the word "neighbor" meant "fellow citizen" and excluded others. The people considered it normal to love their neighbors and hate their enemies (2 Sam. 19:5-6). When Jesus began to live among them, he discovered that this law had been misrepresented and its spirit lost by a popular interpretation: "You shall love your neighbors and hate your enemies" (Matt. 5:43). It no longer reflects the love of God, the Father. Jesus rejected this interpretation because all human beings are "neighbors." He then radicalized it and gave it a new inclusive interpretation with a note of compassion. To clarify what this new interpretation of love means, Jesus tried to differentiate it from the one the people already knew. "You have heard that it was said, you shall love your neighbor and hate your enemy, but I say to you to love your enemies and pray for those who persecute you" (Matt. 5:44). Jesus gives as his reason for this love of our enemies the love of God which knows no bounds. It welcomes both good and bad people. This new interpretation of the law of love has yet to receive popular acceptance.

The word of God has told us to love one another and the reason for doing so.

But how are we to love in a world where any form of ethnic and racial prejudice, sectionalism, and hostility in the sharing and distribution of social amenities, allocation of economic wealth, and employment opposes the love for one another? We live in a society where people love with favor in view, and when such anticipated favors are not forthcoming, the relationship ends. We are living at a time when people claim to love but are full of deceit and lies. We live in a time when the world and society are full of hate, wickedness, and war. We can say that love has often been abused and becomes distorted. Today, the true meaning has become suspect and is approached with doubt and reluctance by some of us. It is common knowledge that we live in a society where the true meaning of love is lost to selfish interest, compromise, or favoritism.

In these and similar societies, love for the enemy goes against what is ingrained in many of us who want justice or revenge in moments of conflict. What is more difficult and, at times, unclear is how to love those who, by their lifestyles and activities, do not love us or deserve to be loved. I mean such people who hurt us individually or collectively. Consider the enemies of human progress who threaten our family, country or even our Church with destruction and death. The challenge to love them is quite enormous. It is opposed to our human view of reality. As a result, it is easier to choose to love only those who love us or those who are likable. While these tendencies are real and pose a great challenge to the commandment of love given to believers by Jesus Christ, the love of God obliges us to love as our heavenly Father loves. Jesus gives a rationale for the love of enemies.

However, the circumstances, the Christian faith obliges us to love people in spite of their behaviors. This is where Christians make a difference. Our founder, Jesus Christ, knows the pain and challenge of loving our enemies and sinners. Saints, both living and dead, have crossed the barriers of impossible love. Joseph forgave his brothers, who sold him into slavery to Potiphar in Egypt and treated them with love. St. Stephen prayed for those who were executing him by stoning (Acts 7:59). The Apostles of non-violence, such as Dr. Martin Luther King Jr., Mahatma Gandhi, and Nelson Mandela, proved that love could be directed at extreme hatred, not counting the gravity of the offense of the perpetrators. All of these individuals are informed and motivated by Jesus and his teaching about the love of the enemy. They did all this in imitation of the heavenly Father whose sun shines on the good and the bad (Matt. 5:45). Jesus wants us to know that what changes the life of people is not so much a collection of truths, not even teaching or preaching but people in whom they can see the truth of the Gospel of love lived, and a belief put into life.

The bedrock for our action in loving our enemies is our duty to imitate Jesus and his Father. Jesus wants us to know that love is good and does not admit evil. Paul teaches us that love does not rejoice at wrong but rejoices at right (1 Cor. 13:6). The love of God calls for forgiveness in the event of offense, not revenge. If retaliation and revenge are to be used to settle cases, the world will be filled with hate, misery, and revenge. As such, love should be developed to enable us to forgive and let go of the evil people commit against us. We must develop a mental attitude that will enable us to love even in difficult circumstances. This is important because war and coercion do not lead to true peace. Those who are silenced by force and intimidation will rise one day to retaliate. Love is needed for lasting peace, as Jesus demonstrated for our salvation. Jesus has everything it takes to fight and overcome his enemies but fails to recognize his right in order to achieve the salvation of the world. Instead, he said: "Father forgive them; for they know not what they do" (Lk. 23:34). Thus, when one's right is not enforced, not because of weakness or fear or coercion but to avoid the evil effects of revenge, one has arisen to the level of the new love Jesus taught his disciples.

It is important to note that Jesus is not enabling evil by his perspective on love.

He is offering us a love that does not count the gravity of the offense of the aggressor but the good that can be achieved by not paying evil with evil. This understanding of love invites us to see our enemies or opponents as misguided neighbors who do not know what they are doing and pray for them. In this case, though our natural tendency may be to fight, hate and make life difficult for our partner after divorce, for example, this love remains even after the divorce or injury has been inflicted on a friend or foe. Is it any wonder why Gandhi and Martin Luther King, Jr. saw Jesus' advice here not as submissive but subversive, aimed at transforming an evil culture by love and non-violence?

So, loving one another may not be easy, but it is possible. To differentiate it from our other familiar sentiments, Jesus teaches us that loving in the Christian context is not the same as liking. Liking is a sentiment toward a person or something considered likable, pleasant, or agreeable. To replace love with like not only make it selfish but also makes it become compartmentalized. This makes love to be exercised among cliques and becomes, by that, a thing for those who belong to us and are, therefore, deserving of our love and concern. Those who do not belong to us can go to blazes. This is why today, our society has become infested with a false view of love.

Against this background, the love that Jesus teaches is all-inclusive. He does not only love people but is very sensitive to their needs. Jesus does not treat us as we deserve but looks for our well-being. The good or bad deeds of people do not deter him.

On the Cross, he died for all people – the deserving and the undeserving. He does not count our trespasses against us but seeks our forgiveness and well-being. The strength to love in this manner comes from Jesus. This is so because Christian love does not come to an end (1 Cor. 13:8) but forgives the evil done.

In fact, Jesus calls us to love our enemy, not because it is natural or practical but because it is right and just. It may not reflect our instinct, but it reflects the character of God.

God loves the world and sends the Son to it out of love. In his letter to the Romans, Paul says that while we were enemies of God, God revealed his love for us by sending his Son to die for us (Rom. 5:8). We are enemies by our disobedience because sin is a revolt against God. So, while it is difficult to think of loving our enemies, God loves us, who were once enemies and often oppose our will and justice by our sins.

So, when Jesus calls us to love our enemies, he asks us to live the life of God.

He does not tell us what he wants us to do but what he, too, did and continues to do. He loves the good and the bad alike. Loving our enemies is a sign of God's unconditional love for the whole world. It is not just because it is practical but because it is right and just to love.

What is right and just is what is noble. To love a husband, wife, parent, friend, or colleague is about doing what is right, what we ought to do. This is what Paul intends to communicate when he teaches: "Owe no one anything, except to love each other, for the one who loves another has fulfilled the law" (Rom. 13:8). When we love for the sake of loving, we do what is right. We give thanks to God by embracing life and the duties he has given us. We see meaning in what we do and live gracefully. Paul echoes a similar principle when he exhorts believers to do and be concerned with "whatever things are true, whatever things are noble, whatever things are just, whatever things are pure, whatever things are lovely, whatever things are of good report, if there is any virtue and if there is anything praiseworthy" (Phil. 4:8). All the "whatevers" point to what is right and just which "love for neighbor" is one of them.

The right thing points to the duties we owe God and humanity in love. A right sense of this love does not focus on how we can hurt ourselves but on doing the right thing even when it hurts. It is good and right to rejoice at suffering when we know that it is because we are doing what is right. Is it any wonder Mother Teresa of Calcutta is often credited with saying that we should continue to "love even when it hurts?"

Thus, love teaches us that the fiber of the Christian faith is in relationships: first with God through Jesus Christ and then with one another without reserve. We may not achieve uniformity in belief, culture, and personality, but we may achieve love and unity in diversity. Realizing this truth after many years of scandalous battle with one another in the name of Christianity, St. John Paul II made a name for himself when he went to the Jewish synagogue in Rome to pray. He was the first bishop of Rome to do so since St. Peter. He called the Jewish people "our brothers, indeed our elder brothers." Pope Francis invited Middle East leaders to pray for peace with him at the Vatican, and they did, even though they belonged to other religions. Inspired by the same light of love and compassion, St. Mother Theresa and like-minded saints took their mission to non-Catholics and non-believers.

In all this, it takes Christian love to make a difference in the world of selfishness, enmity, division, discrimination, and finger-pointing. Is it any wonder Jesus wants us to know that Christian love differentiates Christians' lives from others? "By this all men will know that you are my disciples if you have love for one another" (Jn. 13:35). Jesus wants Christians to make a difference in the world in the spirit of his love expressed through selfless service. Therefore, to be a Christian is to know love, live love, and share the love with one another.

THE IMPLICATION OF LOVE FOR THE CHRISTIAN

As we have noted, our God is love. Experts in religion tell us that people always try to be like the God they worship. People who worship a warrior god tend to be warmongering, people who worship a god of pleasure tend to be pleasure-seeking, people who worship a god of wrath tend to be vengeful, and people who worship a god of love tend to be loving. So, as a god is, so are his worshipers. Christians worship the God who is love (1 Jn. 4:8), and as such, should reflect his love. If God is love, then it has enough implications for believers in Christ. It requires us to acknowledge and testify how much of God's love for us has been personally experienced and internalized. If Jesus is the reflection of the love of the Father, and we are not only co-heirs with Jesus (Rom. 8:17) but also have his Spirit, we should reflect the love of God and Jesus. To do this, we need first to realize how much God loves us and allow that love to permeate and transform us and dispose of us to become the true reflection of the divine love of God in us.

As recipients of the love of God, love is to be who we are and not an appendage to our lives. It is to become not only what we do with our hands, eyes, or lips but who we are as persons. It is not enough to possess it but to be possessed by it. When love possesses us, we are better disposed to love unconditionally. When the core of our being is thus possessed by love, we break with selfishness which is the greatest enemy of love. The core of our being is possessed when the Holy Spirit is given our total person. The Holy Spirit is the love of the Father poured into our hearts. When he possesses us, he rules our entire being with love and inspires us to love. When we are thus possessed and filled, love becomes a way of living, relating, and serving our neighbor.

It means that Christian love is at the service of the other and entails a sacrifice.

Already Jesus has, by the self-giving of himself, taught us that love is a sacrifice, a total giving of oneself spiritually and materially for the good of the other. As he broke the bread of his body on the Cross and gave it to us, he wants us to break the bread of our hearts and talents for the well-being of others. He wants us to love one another with a sense of sacrifice, sensitivity, and selfless service. In imitation of this way of love, we are to see it as part of who we are to use our time, talent, and treasure to help those in need: the homeless, malnourished children, paupers, widows, refugees, and immigrants in our midst. We are to do this without counting the cost, as Jesus did when he gave his life for our salvation without counting the cost. In the spirit of the love Jesus expressed through selfless service, we are to make a difference in the world of labor by rendering our services in our different places of work, not necessarily to earn money but to enhance the joy of humanity and make the burden of life bearable.

When we see love as a sacrifice, we no longer expect gratitude to love people over and over again. This is important because, at times, we decide not to give up our love just because those we helped have not called to thank us for good deeds done or showed gratitude.

As a matter of fact, when we join our love with the sacrificial love of Jesus, we do not expect a human reward for our acts of love. There is no problem accepting gratitude when a beneficiary offers it, but it should not be a reason for loving or giving gifts to our neighbor. This is the root of Jesus' banquet invitation toward the poor, the disabled, the lame, and the blind who can never repay kindness (Lk. 14:12-13). Our love is to be reckless, thinking nothing of return or cost except the good of the neighbor, even and especially when the beneficiaries fail to realize the sacrifice involved. Jesus did not give his life for us because we love him or would show gratitude but because he is love and cannot but love.

With these implications, we see why Christians should love by all means. It is because to be Christian is to love with the love of Christ. It is because to be Christian is to share in the love of God. God's relationship with us leaves us with his love. One can never realize this love and not be compelled to share it with others. In other words, by its nature, one cannot realize genuine love and keep it to oneself. Those who find it difficult to love, do not lack love but choose not to love. They acknowledge the love of God for them but fail to realize it personally. That is to say that they are yet to realize how much God loves them. It is our Christian vocation to know God's love, accept it for what it is, and allow it to pervade our humanity and personality. When it does, it is no longer abstract knowledge but an experiential one that flows like a river in our hearts and motivates us to love our neighbor. If we do not realize the love of God for us, we cannot love unconditionally. This is so because the self-giving love of Jesus is the basis for our Christian love.

With love, we make God, who is love, present. This is why John teaches us that anyone who loves is of God and shares in God (1 Jn. 4:7). To love the other then is to love God. In this way, love becomes a means of making God available when we love one another. In expressing love with one another, we share not only our oneness but our equality before God. As a universal love that draws its inspiration from the way Christ loves us, Christian love looks at people from God's point of view, recognizes their dignity as people created in the image of God, and treats everyone with respect. It is love that recognizes that the other is a distinct personality with a distinct history and a distinct set of abilities who needs to be treated with respect and care. We need and are needed by the other person. We do not need to go far to realize that whenever we have grown beyond our immaturity and limitations, it has been through the influence of the other person as a parent, a friend, a priest, a coach, or a teacher. It is by their sacrificial love in service.

CONCLUSION

So, for Christians, love is indispensable. We are created and redeemed by love and endowed with love in and through the Holy Spirit. We live and breathe in love.

The love of God holds us in being. It is our life and what we do. It so permeates our lives that it becomes our identity. It is the driving force of our activity and ministry.

As those who share in the dignity of God by our share of grace, Christians live in imitation of the boundless love of Jesus and not by human love, which is punctuated by self-interest, manipulation, discrimination, and greed. The Christian is called to love because it is the core of Christian living. He is to love with a deep sense of motivation and a clear goal.

Christian love is different from romantic love, which is expressed in feelings. It is not a principle but something we can feel, see, touch, exercise, and share. Its goal is to serve human needs and to improve humanity. Therefore, as we do our daily work, let us strive to make a difference in the world through our Christian love. The greatest homage we can pay to the Christian faith is to live in such a way that through us, people begin to glimpse the unbounded and unconditional love God has shown us in Christ. By this way of love, friends, families, well-wishers, and fellows show that we are disciples of Jesus.

So, with Jesus, we come to know that to live in love is to make oneself a sacrifice for a great cause. It is to see love as the total giving of oneself for the glory of God and the good of others. It is to be proactive in our love and use it to create connections and build bridges between people. This is what Jesus does as our mediator before God. Just as he is a link between God and his people, he wants us to realize that we are, by love, a link in a connection chain between persons. Therefore, as Christians, let us use all the opportunities that come our way to brighten the world with the love of Christ poured into our hearts.

> For if you forgive other people when they sin against you, your heavenly Father will also forgive you.

Matthew 6:14

CHAPTER 6

IT IS A LIFE LIVED BY
Forgiveness

We are created as sons and daughters of one God to live as brothers and sisters in love and harmony. At times efforts to love and be loved are weighed down as we offend or are offended and lose face. While we may desire to love everybody and seek the well-being of all, our human nature often reveals its weakness and puts our relationships in a bad spot. Anger and disputes against brothers and sisters become commonplace, and our relationships become sour. Jesus knows this and teaches his disciples and those who are to become Christians to restore our strained relationships by forgiveness.

The problem is not that we can love or be at odds with one another but that when we are offended, anger does not allow us to forgive because anger and unforgiveness are intertwined. While forgiveness, by its definition, is the giving up of resentment against someone who has hurt us, anger, on the other hand, is the storing of resentment against someone who has hurt us. This is why you cannot understand forgiveness unless you understand the anger.

HOW DOES ANGER MAKE FORGIVENESS DIFFICULT?

Anger, as an emotion, is a strong feeling of intense displeasure, hostility, or indignation as a result of a real or imagined threat to self-esteem or to insult, injustice, physical harm, or injury towards us or others who are dear to us. When we are angry and do not ignore or let it go, we store it in our memory. The anger we store is responsible for conscious or unconscious physical reactions and depression. This is so because the stored anger makes its victim become a store of bitterness. It makes the victim (you or me) act like a pot of boiling water or a carbonated drink. It so fills one's emotional state with the steam of displeasure that it erupts with ease at any slight provocation. "I don't know why John likes to get on my nerves." "Get out of here. You are good for nothing." Expressions of this kind come out of the vapor of the spoken words of an angry person.

Some of us live with a list, written in our minds or on paper, of people we believe have wronged, hurt, misused, misjudged, or mistreated us. Sometimes, there are no specific names of people who have offended us; rather, what we have may be a generalized feeling of bitterness. Our anger may come from our wrong judgment and misinterpretation of actions. As soon as anything happens with people on our list, we voice our anger; we express our stored anger; we become enraged. One may deny he is angry but cannot erase the evidence from his face.

All this goes to confirm that anger is an emotion. It is a signal of a feeling that we are being treated unfairly. In fact, feelings are great sources of anger and often inform our perception, interpretation, and action. As a feeling, psychologists say that anger is neither right nor wrong. In other words, *it is okay* to feel angry. But that is not true. Those who say there is nothing wrong with anger need to rethink. Anger is like fire. No one plays with it, or else it burns. It has caused much harm to human life. Today we see the effects of anger everywhere. The world and the people in it are full of anger. This shows itself on the faces of people we meet, the rate of suicide and homicide in our country, national and international conflicts, relational conflicts, backbiting, divorce, and the present-day indiscriminate litigations.

Unfortunately, we accuse this widespread anger on the situation of things around us. But situations do not produce anger. Anger comes from the way we look at what has happened. You and I produce our own anger. It comes from how we see, perceive, and interpret things. It also comes from what we feel and think about the offender: his nonchalant attitude, lack of remorse, arrogance, or lies, may be what leads to resentment. So, anger is personal. It is my response to situations and the attitudes of people that are unacceptable to me. It is my response to wrongs done to the people I love or me. In reality, things do not make us angry, instead, we choose to be angry. Often, we hear someone say: "Insult makes me angry." If you have decided that it makes you angry, you store it in your head. Any day or time you let it out, it is not the insult causing you to be angry, but you are acting out what you stored in your memory. One can say that you choose to be angry. In the same way you choose anger, you could also choose humor or laugh at it and treat it as nothing.

In fact, nobody makes us angry. We do not catch anger like fire but by a feeling of dislike. We generate our anger by what we are thinking. If you think of an angry thought, you entertain anger in your mind. Your irrational thoughts kick off a battle about whether the other person is fair or not. Angry thoughts will grow with the *intention* you give to them. Our thoughts are the cause, and the effect is our anger. When you hold on to crazy thoughts, you begin to do crazy things just as you do peaceful things when you hold on to peaceful thoughts. In this way, anger is what you and I do, not what happens to us.

A sequel to thinking is belief. Belief can motivate anger. It is what I believe about what has happened that makes me store or express my anger. The belief that an offender needs to be punished, or the belief that somebody needs to pay for his mistakes, or a belief in a tooth for a tooth and an eye for an eye, or the belief in penalty and revenge determines my response to offense and forgiveness.

One of the personal understandings we have about anger that perpetuates it is the belief that anger is natural. But the truth is that anger is habitual and not natural. Anger is usually learned from parents, family members, or a beloved teacher or friend. The way our parents handle anger and forgiveness forms and informs us. Sometimes we act out our parents' angry responses to things and people. Have you ever asked why we deny our anger? It is because it is a habit. The moment we get used to anger by day-to-day responses to our situations, we no longer see or recognize what we do as coming from anger. Mario once asked his daughter: "Angie, if you were asked what you would like to change about me, what would you say?" "Dad, it is your yelling," answered the daughter. Mario told Angie, "My family yells, but my wife's family does not. I have stopped yelling since I got married because my wife does not yell." "Dad," said Angie, "that is not true. You yell a lot." The truth is that Mario is far from where his wife is. He still needs conversion, but he does not realize it!

The awareness we need to have about anger is that there is nothing good about it, and to hold on to it is not good because it is destructive to health and relationships. When we fail to forgive, we carry our accusations about that person in our minds. The constant rehearsing of the sin of the other and associating that person with it whenever he is mentioned robs our hearts of joy and keeps the mind restless. Our bitterness does not only threaten and hurt our health; it threatens the divine presence in our life. This is so because cultivating and brooding over anger opens oneself up to demonic contamination and attack. The devil preys on anger to master the victim. Don't let him have the opportunity by saying no to anger. Do not let the sun go down on your anger because the devil will get a mighty foothold on your soul (Eph. 4:27).

Unfortunately, we do not quite realize that anger is deceptive. Often, what we know is the wrongs that some people have done or are doing to us, but we do not know the harm we are doing to ourselves by our anger and unforgiveness. It is important to remember that any time we forgive, we do not only set free or release the culprit; we release ourselves.

But when we fail, we hold ourselves at ransom. In other words, forgiveness is a gift shared by the offended and the offender.

The fact is that when you do not want to forgive, it is because you are holding on to your anger. Holding on to anger with somebody is like taking poison and wishing the other person to die. In a real sense, it is the angry person who "will die" of the poison instead of the enemy for whom he holds the anger. This is another way of saying that anger causes harm to the one who is keeping it rather than the offender. In fact, holding on to anger makes you bring bitterness into every relationship you have with people. Is it any wonder why it brings alienation, division, separation, and divorce? This is why Sirach tells us that the angry person hugs rage (27:30) and does not have peace. The implication is that when anger overtakes its victim, it becomes a reason for unforgiveness. This is so because unforgiveness makes its victims live in anger.

The emphasis here is that unforgiving spirit does not build but destroys, divides families, ruins friendships, splits churches, and poisons communities. It is natural to be angry when something goes wrong, but the problem comes when anger grows into resentment, bitterness, and hostility. When this happens, the whole person is consumed and imprisoned by anger. All too often, extreme anger is infected with hate. Although we may claim that we only hate certain ideas, orientations, tenets, or particular deeds, it is easy to slip from hating ideas into hating the people who hold them. It is no longer only anger, but hate driven by anger. There is no limit to the evil anger can cause to its victims.

However, the problem with anger is that an angry person does not believe he is angry. When we deny it or justify it, we perpetuate it. Hence Paul invites us to get rid of all bitterness and rage and extinguish the fire of anger and live (Eph. 4:31). Perpetuating your anger makes you remain a killer to yourself and others (Matt. 5:21-22). In this text, Jesus equates anger with murder because anger can be the precursor to murder. Therefore, it is important to heed James, who admonishes us to be slow to anger (1:19-20) because anger is a sin (Col. 3:8).

WHY IS FORGIVENESS NECESSARY?

Forgiveness is the giving up of resentment against someone and our right to get even what has been done to us. It is the surrendering of my right to hurt my offender back. It is God's established way of dealing with strained relationships. It is the character of God, who is loving and slow to anger abounding in mercy (Ps. 103:8; Ex 34:6, Lam 3:22-23), who calls us to be compassionate as he is compassionate (Lk. 6:36). It is true that forgiveness may not change the misdeeds of the past. It does change the power of the past to control our present and future life and activities. This may be why Paul calls us to forgive our grievances against one another (Col. 3:13), as the Lord forgives us.

Forgiveness is divine, life-giving, and aids relationships. It is necessary because each one of us needs a relationship. No one of us lives for ourselves (Rom. 14:7). This means we cannot survive without relationships. No matter the stuff we are made of, we need one another.

Since human weakness always makes it difficult to experience healthy relationships, forgiveness then becomes a way of healing strained relationships. In other words, healthy relationships are good for a healthy life. The opposite, a strained relationship, affects our health and life.

As a matter of fact, resentment as a deep-seated anger is toxic and corrodes our human systems. The damage such a chronic emotional state can do to our health is enormous. Before you know it, it begins to breed depression, sadness, and insensitivity. When this happens, the person gradually becomes isolated and miserable as people find it difficult to relate with him at the level of his negativity. This way of living brings the heart and mind to the risks of huge sickness. But some psychologists say that forgiveness is good for our hearts and lowers our blood pressure and stress.

Forgiveness liberates believers from the clutches of Satan. An angry man's heart is the devil's workshop in the way that only evil thoughts resonate incessantly in it. As a result, anger creates an opening through which the evil one can operate. Since Satan's secret weapon is unforgiveness and the absence of love, whenever unforgiveness and bitterness enter our hearts, we give Satan a legal right to build his stronghold within us. Paul tells the Corinthian Christians that when we withhold forgiveness, we give Satan a potential advantage over us (2 Cor. 2:10-11). No wonder then he warns the Ephesians with such urgency: "Let all bitterness, wrath, anger…, with all malice, be put away from you. And be kind to one another, forgiving one another, even as God in Christ forgave you" (Eph. 4:31-32). So, forgiveness not only breaks the cycle of revenge; it also saves those who forgive from the infestation of Satan.

One other reason for forgiveness is our human frailty. The unjust aggressor inflicts injury to his victims from human weakness. We, humans, are weak by nature and can make mistakes from our shortcomings. As such, we are more disposed to pity the sinner and to forgive when we honestly acknowledge our weaknesses. Those who know they are weak and accept it see their oppressors as misled neighbors who do not know what they are doing and pray for them as Jesus did. As a matter of fact, we all are sinners in need of forgiveness. "If we say we have no sin, we deceive ourselves, and the truth is not in us. If we confess our sins, he is faithful and just and will forgive our sins and cleanse us from all unrighteousness. If we say we have not sinned, we make him a liar, and his word is not in us" (1 Jn. 1:8-10). This realization can offer us a great help to forgive because we, too, can make mistakes and stand in need of forgiveness. It is important to understand that acknowledging our weakness does not condone sin but shows the necessity for forgiveness.

Is it any wonder God, our Creator, commands that forgiveness be granted to our neighbors? Because God forgives us and commands us to do likewise is a reason to ponder its necessity. Even when we feel we cannot forgive the offender for any reason, we still forgive because God freely forgives us of our sins (Matt. 6: 12). It then becomes our duty in love as those who receive forgiveness from God to forgive our neighbor. God does not distinguish between the sins to forgive and the ones not to forgive. He tells us to forgive our neighbor as He forgives us. In this way, we can forgive for the sake of God. Even when our offender does not deserve forgiveness, God deserves our obedience to his command. We are to forgive not only because the Lord has forgiven us but as the Lord has forgiven us. His forgiveness was costly, not cheap. It cost him his life. As recipients of God's love and forgiveness, we should not fail to forgive just because it will cost us a lot to do. We should not be concerned with what it is going to cost us to forgive others. To imitate Christ and the way of the cross is to realize that forgiveness is full and final, not partial or provisional. It is free. Jesus wants his disciples to learn to forgive freely with his lengthy teaching on relationships and fraternal correction of an erring brother or sister. Because our heavenly Father is a forgiving God, we strive to be of the same mind as him. In Jesus Christ, who calls him Father, we see the love and mercy of God. If we acknowledge him as our Father, we must bear his love and mercy and heed his command to forgive our neighbor.

HOW OFTEN MUST I FORGIVE?

In the Old Testament, the rabbis had a general rule of thumb that indicated a sinner could be forgiven as many as three times. Unfortunately, these rabbis fixed this limit from an erroneous interpretation of Amos 1:3 and 2:1. "Thus, says the Lord: 'For three transgressions of Damascus, and for four, I will not revoke the punishment, because they have threshed Gilead with threshing sledges of iron.'" In other words, Damascus could be pardoned for her sins three times but would not be shown pity for a fourth offense. This would have been considered very generous and merciful among the Jews, who were very fond of defining and limiting moral obligations as if they could be accurately prescribed by number.

Influenced by this numbering tradition, Peter came up to Jesus one day to ask, "Lord, how often shall my brother sin against me, and I forgive him? As many as seven times?" (Matt. 18:21-22). Peter suggested to Jesus that a community member who sins against another should be forgiven as many as seven times. In his response, "Jesus said to him, I do not say to you seven times, but seventy times seven" (Matt. 18:22). This is a symbolic way of saying that a sinner must be forgiven an indefinite number of times. With this, Christ demolished the attempt to define by law the measure of grace or to quantify it.

But there is more to Peter's intention than the number. The suggestion about "how much forgiveness is required for a brother" is not only a desire to set limits to forgiveness but a desire to know when his anger with his brother is justifiable. He wanted to know what limits were to be imposed on his generosity, especially if the offender made no reparation for his offense or acknowledged not his wrongdoing. Having familiarized himself with the tradition of forgiving only three times, Peter felt that he was raising the bar substantially by suggesting to Jesus that a community member who sins against another should be forgiven as many as seven times. This is double the generosity offered by the rabbis. Seven is the number of completeness and plurality. Our Lord had used it when he spoke about forgiveness: "Even if they sin against you seven times in a day and seven times come back to you saying, 'I repent,' you must forgive them" (Lk. 17:4). Peter would be shocked to hear Jesus correct the number of times a sinner must be forgiven to "seventy times seven times." In other words, a sinner must be forgiven an indefinite number of times. In this case, forgiveness is not so much what we do but an attitude to be integrated into our way of thinking and living.

Like Peter, we do not only want to place limits on the number of times we should decline to forgive but what types of sins we should not forgive. Should we forgive homicide and infidelity in marriage? How about the sins of kidnappers and rapists who leave scars and bruises of abuse in the lives of people we love? Do they deserve to love those who pounded the nails into the flesh of Jesus when he did no wrong to them? Unfortunately, Jesus does not give any distinction between the sins to forgive and the ones not to forgive. He just tells us to forgive our neighbor as God forgives us (Matt. 6:12). In this way, we can forgive for the sake of God, even when our offender does not deserve our forgiveness. It means to be merciful by withholding the punishment meant for someone who deserves it or is in need.

CONCLUSION

Like the Jewish community, we live, work, study, pray, and trade side by side with people of different upbringings and cultures. Every week the media is full of accounts of terrible acts committed by people in retaliation or revenge for something done against them, real or imagined. Many of us live with a list, written in our minds if not on paper, of people we believe have wronged, abused, cheated, or mistreated us. Sometimes there are no specific names but generalized feelings of bitterness or anger that erupt in unpredictable ways. There is not even one of us who does not have something to forgive or some things for which we need forgiveness. How could anyone then survive without forgiveness?

Therefore, unmindful of how much the offense may be, the Lord recommends forgiveness to Christians. By forgiveness, the Christian chooses to pardon, remit, or overlook the offender's mistake, fault, offense, hurt, or injury without demanding a penalty, punishment, or retribution. This is a great need because the world is joined together by relationships and love. At times, a relationship is treated with selfishness. It then becomes commonplace that living together can provoke offense and disappointment. There is no other way to live peacefully except to forgive offense or be reconciled as Jesus asks us to do in his teachings.

However, "forgiveness," it must be admitted, "is not easy." It is one of the toughest aspects of our Christian practice. It is not easy to forgive the person who injured or abused you without asking for forgiveness. It is difficult to forgive the person who offended you and still threatens to deal with you. It is not easy to forgive the person who killed one of your beloved relations! It is not easy to forgive the person who falsely accused you of what you did not do and, in the process, presents a false image of you to the public. Forgiving your kidnapper, rapist, abusive spouse, or employer is not easy. In fact, we have a natural tendency for revenge. At times, the action that breaks our relationship often leaves scars on our bodies or wounds in our hearts. We can go on and on to give different kinds of things that can make forgiveness difficult. One thing is certain, these and similar situations may make forgiveness difficult to handle but not impossible.

If then forgiveness is not impossible, and as Christians, we cannot but forgive. The question now is not what type or number of sins to forgive but to know what forgiveness is not. Forgiveness is not condoning wrongdoing or ignoring its gravity. It is not condoning evil but destroying evil. It is not a sign of weakness but of strength. It is not a sign of cowardice but courage. It does not depend on the wrongdoer's repentance (Lk. 23:34) or apology. It is not a sign that the evil deeds of the offender have been righted or justified but have been forgiven.

The mystery of life we are required to meditate about here is that it takes a human to offend and a human to be offended. We would not be human if we did not feel anger now and then when displeased. But we should not allow our anger to unpack its bags and build a home in us because of our unforgiveness. Hence, Jesus asks us to forgive from our hearts. He makes it clear that there is no limit to giving and receiving forgiveness for all who accept the kingdom of God in their lives.

The message for Christians today is that if God has shown mercy to us by granting us pardon for our sins, then we, in turn, must show mercy and forgiveness toward every person who has offended us. If we expect God to pardon us and show us his mercy when we sin and disobey his commandments, we must be willing to let go of any resentment or ill will we feel towards our neighbor. An offense is always present in the spirit of the person who does not want or know how to let time act, the time that inexorably passes and that allows offenses to be forgotten. This is important because the single remedy that allows the forgiveness of offenses is time. But time does not wait for anyone. The earlier we let go and forgive, the better. Often, forgiveness delayed is forgiveness denied and punishment exerted. This is why Jesus answers Peter by saying that he must repeatedly forgive, up to seventy-seven times, thus giving *time* a chance to act and allowing the offense to disappear from memory.

In this case, forgiveness calls for the renewal of a mindset inherited while growing up. It calls for a change from selfishness, vindictiveness, and a heart of stone. A true Christian allows his heart to be formed after the heart of Christ's love and his mind after the mind of Christ. Jesus calls us to form our "conscience," to be motivated by love and forgiveness, and to embrace one another as God's children. To live in a community, then, is to learn how to love and how to forgive offenses. Therefore, to be a Christian is to receive forgiveness and to forgive those who sin against us.

> If you abide in me, and my
> words abide in you, ask for
> whatever you wish, and
> it will be done for you.

John 15:7

CHAPTER 7

IT IS A LIFE OF
Prayer & Worship

rayer is one of the greatest expressions of religion. There is no religion that does not have a form of prayer by means of which adherents worship their God or gods. The first thing children remember most about their parents' religion is prayer. The prayer life of their parents or grandparents often informs and forms how they pray. The place of prayer in worship is so much emphasized that many people believe that prayer is everything in religion. To pray well is understood by some as practicing religion well. As a result, Christianity loses its meaning as a religion of life and becomes a religion of prayer. In this way, some undue emphasis is laid more on prayer than on Christian life.

Wherever this emphasis exists, prayer is often seen as an indulgence to be gained after going through some novenas, devotions, or observing a specific number of petitions.

This distorted perspective makes praying empty and laborious. In contradistinction, prayer is packed with grace because it is an encounter with God. The time spent in prayer may be conceived of as a time of grace or a covenantal moment of grace. It is wrong when one makes prayer be seen as an activity that we ought to do for so and so number to convince God, while prayer is, in fact, a state of being in which we celebrate the grace of God through what we give or receive.

As a matter of fact, for some Christians, prayer is what we run to when something is wrong or during difficult moments. When you share your problem with people, the quickest response to it is "take it to God in prayer." This approach to prayer has eaten deep into our psyche so that we do not only pray unmindfully but also pray as if prayer is a magic wand that gives an automatic response to every problem of life. While it is good to pray and to invite God to every life situation, it is important to realize that while prayer is powerful and efficacious, it also requires a good atmosphere, the right disposition, faith, and aligning our will to the will of God. Prayer is not just a matter of talking but an encounter with God.

While prayer is on the lips of every child of God, some of us do not know what prayer is or how to pray. Some of the things we know about prayer are wrongly learned or presumed. As a result, prayer becomes a mere heaping up of concerns. Against the erroneous way of seeing prayer as where we go to heap up our concerns, this reflection undertakes to share that prayer begins with a desire to experience God, to visit with God, and to be with God. The psalmist brings out this earnest desire and longing for divine presence by expressing how he seeks earnestly, thirsts or yearns, and longs for the presence of God (Pss. 63:1; 143:6; 42:2).

"My soul longs, yea, faints, for the courts of the Lord; my heart and my flesh cry out for the living God" (Ps. 84:2). In all this, we see earnest desire, intimate longing, and readiness to communicate with God.

As Paul also calls it, this earnest desire for divine presence comes from a deep-rooted relationship or conversion experience. In this way, prayer can be said to be the celebration of the relationship between God as a Father and his people. As such, it does not only take place within the context of a father-child relationship; it is a sharing motivated and nourished by love, fondness, trust, and a deep sense of care. God does not just create, but as a father, loves and takes care of his sons and daughters. He lavishes them with promises of continued love, care, providence, and protection: "Call upon me in the time of trouble; I will deliver you, and you shall glorify me" (Ps. 50:15); "Fear not, for I am with you, be not dismayed, for I am your God; I will strengthen you, I will help you; I will uphold you with my victorious right hand" (Is. 41:10). In promises of this kind, God demonstrates his affection, care, protection, and nearness to his children.

The good news here is that prayer is about relationships. In this relationship, God's will is accepted, and a responsible lifestyle is cultivated. This forms the basis on which confidence is built, words chosen, and feelings freely expressed because Jesus encourages us to be bold in prayer and makes demands based on the special and loving "Father-child" relationship God has with us.

But loving relationships do not simply happen by what we do at the impulse of the moment. Instead, they are built up, step by step, brick by brick, and layer by layer over time. The father and son or daughter know each other and spend quality time together. They care about each other with a great sense of concern and affection. They love, work, talk, and listen to each other with delight, fondness, and appreciation. Similarly, our long-time relationship with God makes for a deeply loving commitment and trust. In a relationship of this kind, prayers are articulated, trusted, and answered. As a matter of fact, when this disposition is cultivated, it makes prayer a celebration, an expression of bond, an oasis of security and comfort, a sanctuary replete with favors, a rekindling of love, a source of courage, a reaffirming of trust and a balm of empowerment.

So, familial sentiments accompany a father-child relationship. Good parents are known for reading their children's body language well and can anticipate their children's needs. As a father, God does not only love with everlasting love, but he is also constant in his affection for his children. Expressing this affection of a parent, God said to Isaiah: "Can a woman forget her nursing child or show no compassion for the child of her womb? Even these may forget, yet I will not forget you" (49:15). God will not forget because he delights in our well-being and is ready to give up anything for our sake.

As is common with relationships, we do not learn how to pray better; we become better children of prayer when our relationship with God becomes more intimate as that of father and child. In this way, we no longer see prayer as a stereotype, a fixed construct, or "business as usual" but spontaneous as the time and situation may determine. This means that one of the ways to develop intimacy in our prayer life is by creating a culture of praying always.

Following this relationship, we see prayer also as communion. It provides an opportunity for believers and God to commune together. When this kind of relationship exists between a child and parent, the child becomes fond of his father and always desires his father's company. In like manner, our friendly ties with God dispose us to desire his company and commune and talk with him. In such a prayer we make ourselves available and stay aware of God's presence. We establish an encounter. In this moment of encounter and sharing, we experience genuine security and feel the intimacy of being a child of God and the transforming power that comes through fellowship with him. We engage in a continuous, open-ended conversation with God. It is important to know that God wants to be included in every activity, conversation, challenge, and thought. This is what Paul implies when he says, "And whatever you do, in word or deed, do everything in the name of the Lord Jesus, giving thanks to God the Father through him" (Col. 3:17). This is the essence of all prayer, namely, communion with God.

In this communion, we do not pray to change God's mind or necessarily to get things or make things happen. We pray to be in communion with God, who alone knows what is good for us and gives freely to us. In this manner of praying, we go about our daily work in a spirit of communion with God. The harmony of this communion transforms our whole being to the extent that whether we are praising, worshiping, singing, asking, celebrating, or adoring, what matters is to be in communion with the Lord. What is important is that it is an encounter with the Lord. In fact, to establish communion is to make prayer part of who we are, our true life.

If prayer is about relationship and communion with God, all it means is that love, trust, and assurance are at the root and center of Christian prayer. When we fall in love, our trust and sense of goodwill for the one we love become our concern. From the depth of this sense of concern, we develop a meeting to share our sentiments of love, assurance, promise, and relentless support. We can assure each other of concern thus: "If there is anything you think I can do to help you, do not hesitate to call or ask me." With a promise of this kind, we bring our friend to partake of our joy and our benefaction. In so doing, we create a meeting point of shared concern. Similarly, God invites us to enjoy his presence and goodness in prayer. The scriptures are full of God's promises of protection, favor, comfort, companionship, help, guidance, providence, mercy, love, and deliverance, to mention but a few. The Christian is not only surrounded by these shades of God's benevolence, but prayer is a veritable means of appropriating divine benevolence to oneself. With scriptural promises, God makes clear to us his love and gives us the key to open and share in his riches through prayer.

Again, if prayer is about relationship and communion with God, it is then a family affair and an indispensable part of the Christian life. Like our earthly parents who are involved in our affairs, God wants to hear us speak and talk to us. Therefore, when we pray, he makes Himself available and listens. Through prayer, we open our hearts to him: our fears and doubts, joys and sorrows, and allow him to work in us and through us. He touches us at the points of our needs, and we touch and feel his power, presence, and goodness. As a Father who is involved in the affairs of his children, he does much more than we ask and pray. As he put it, "When you pass through the waters, I will be with you; and through the rivers, they shall not overwhelm you; when you walk through the fire, you shall not be burned, and the flame shall not consume you" (Is. 43:2). In prayer we articulate our faith and awareness of God's involvement in our affairs. We celebrate our familial sentiments, experience the touch of the divine embrace, and feel the warmth of belongingness.

Prayer can further be said to be a kind of offertory, a sacrifice we make of ourselves and our actions. Thus, understood, we turn our obedience and faithfulness into sacrifices we offer to God. In this way, we offer our lives, our intentions, wishes, dreams, fears, and actions as fragrant offerings to God to live for him. In other words, we allow the things we do to speak to God on our behalf without having to voice our needs. This is so because sacrifice is a prayer of action. We engage in this prayer with our works of charity or corporal works of mercy. Our charity, when offered to the glory of God and the well-being of his needy people, is a prayer of sacrifice. It goes to mean that good deeds beget blessings. "Because you have done this, I will bless you" (Gen. 22:12-19). Is it any wonder why Mass is the highest form of prayer, made by Jesus Christ, the perfect victim of our salvation? In him and with him, our everyday participation in any gift of charity, devotion, praise, and thanksgiving that aids in changing a person's nature from self-centeredness is a sacrifice, a prayer. "Through him then let us continually offer up a sacrifice of praise to God, that is, the fruit of lips that acknowledge his name" (Heb. 13:15).

So, prayer is one of the ways Christians live out their religious life. It is a loving encounter between God and humanity. It is a meeting point in which humans encounter the saving power of the Lord, which transforms, liberates, heals, encourages, and aids in times of need. Whether God or the human person initiates this encounter, prayer creates a divine environment. It provokes a communion with the Divine; through it, information passes from one to the other with verbal and mental conjectures.

JESUS AND PRAYER

Jesus did not define prayer, but his prayer life and teachings on prayer are enough insight into what prayer means to him. He started his ministry with prayer and ended it with prayer. While it was still dark, he woke up early in the morning to go to a lonely place where he prayed (Mk. 1:35). He prayed for the healing of the sick, the deliverance of those possessed by the devil, and the raising of the dead. He prayed for the protection of his disciples from the evil one and from division (Jn. 17:11) as well as those who will believe in him through their message (Jn. 17:21). He said a prayer of praise to God (Lk. 10:21) and thanksgiving (Mk. 14:22). He also said a prayer of total surrender to the will of God, his Father, during his agony and crucifixion (Matt. 26:39). In the garden of Gethsemane, when he was facing his imminent death, Jesus prayed so earnestly that his sweat became like drops of blood falling to the ground (Lk. 22:44) asking for the will of God even at his own expense. At the darkest hour of his agony on the cross (23:34), while wrestling internally, he entrusted his soul into the hands of God in earnest prayer and finally prayed for the forgiveness of those who caused his suffering and death. In some of these references, we see that Jesus had a life of prayer and prayed in season and out of season. He taught his disciples how to pray.

Though he is God, Jesus prayed throughout his ministry. Found in human form, Jesus prayed incessantly to the Father during times of need. He began every major thing he did with prayer. When the disciples saw his prayer life and how he expressed his relationship with his Father in prayer, they approached and asked him to teach them how to pray. In reply to their request, Jesus taught them a new form of prayer with five components that highlight the right dispositions for Christian prayer:

1. Familial disposition which makes one see prayer as a family affair.

2. Reverential disposition, which shows itself in veneration and worship of God.

3. Disposition to the reign of God.

4. Blameless disposition, which allows one to pray with a heart free from fault.

5. Disposition of total surrender to the will of God.

Our failure to realize and provide for these dispositions makes it difficult for most prayers to achieve their purpose.

According to the teachings of Jesus, prayer springs from a deep relationship with God. It is not a mere articulation of sentiments or a heaping up of words of petition but a celebration of a loving relationship. It rests clearly on a relationship between God and the one praying. In his presentation on prayer, Jesus teaches us that God is a Father. "Fatherhood" bespeaks an intimacy similar to that experienced by a parent and child. As such, the "Our Father" is a prayer based on familiarity. It is a prayer of one who knows he is an heir and joint heir with Christ to the riches of God (Rom. 8:17). It is a prayer of one who is not a stranger to the house of God. So, the prayer of the Christian, like the prayer of Christ, is one patterned in relationship with God the Father.

By asking us to address God as "Our Father," Jesus lifts us from our human domain to the divine domain to share in the dignity that belongs to God. The dignity of God's sons and daughters gives us the courage to enter the sanctuary of God and commune with him, crying Abba, Father (Rom. 8:15-16). In other words, prayer is a family affair based on a relationship of familiarity and love. It is an activity that flows out of an intimate relationship. It is not something we embark upon only when we are in trouble or have no personal relationship with the Lord. It flows from the heart of a child of God who is convinced of his faith and place in God as Father.

So, to pray as Christians is to put ourselves in a situation where we see God as Father and speak to him as his children. We all know that when children speak to their parents, there is hardly a right or wrong way. They put into words or body language what they feel in their hearts. They do not have any inhibitions but are very transparent. They refuse to take no for an answer. Children have the audacity like that Jesus commended in the widow who came to the king to vindicate her against her adversary. "I tell you, even though he will not get up and give you the bread because of friendship, yet because of your sheer audacity, he will surely get up and give you as much as you need" (Lk. 11:8). Jesus uses this interplay between the widow and the judge to teach us about the disposition that opens the door of grace in prayer. It is an irresistible bold disposition. If you say no to a child today, he comes back tomorrow with the same request. We can say that children are shameless and can request anything at any time. They are not moved even when we laugh at what they say and how they put it. They are very optimistic, inquisitive, and level-headed about their needs and what they want.

Just as children can be relentless in their questions and persistent in requests, Jesus teaches us, as God's children, to show the same spirit of perseverance of the request of a child to his father in our prayer to our Father, God. He invites us to approach God with childlike innocence and trust with the assurance that God loves us and delights to give us what is good. As the psalmist put it, "God delights in the well-being of his servants" (Ps. 35:27). As Jesus said in another place, "Do not be afraid, little flock, for it is your Father's good pleasure to give you the kingdom" (Lk. 12:32). This attitude to prayer does not mean reckless audacity that will bring a curse but one that brings blessing. In our prayer, therefore, we should remember that a father asks for familial love, trust, confidence, and sincerity from his children more than a teacher asks from a pupil. "Do you believe that I am able to do this?" asks Jesus (Matt. 9:28).

In the second disposition, Jesus teaches us that prayer begins with a deep sense of honor, reverence, and worship of the holy Name of God.

In other words, prayer celebrates and honors the immense dignity of the great Name of God. According to this disposition, the first thing in prayer is to hallow the Name of God. God has many titles but only one name: YHWH "I AM who I AM." To hallow something is to hold it sacred and holy or set it apart for holy use.

Jesus wants us to realize here that the name of God we call in prayer is holy. We do not make it holy, but it is holy in itself. The name of God speaks of the character of God; it is not something external but something intrinsic to his personality. This is why we must never, in the words of the commandment, "take the Name of the Lord in vain." God revealed his name so that we may use it to call upon his power and draw closer to him in communion. When we call upon the name of the Lord, we remind God of his special relationship with us and our deep sense of trust and honor. So, prayer begins with acknowledging that the Name of the Lord we invoke is holy and deserves to be honored. This is to be shown in the use of words and comportment in prayer.

To hallow the holy name of God is to give it glory. As such, "hallowed be thy name" is the end of all requests. It means that whatever we desire and pray for in prayer for ourselves, or others must be subordinate to this end, namely, the glory of God the Father. Is it any wonder why Jesus said to his disciples: "Let your light so shine before men, that they may see your good works and give glory to your Father who is in heaven?" (Matt. 5:16). The glory of the Lord is also confirmed by Paul as the end of the name of Jesus; "that at the name of Jesus, every knee should bow, in heaven and on earth and under the earth, and every tongue confess that Jesus Christ is Lord, to the glory of God the Father" (Phil. 2:10-11). Paul further says that our desire for daily bread and drink demands that God be glorified in our comfortable use of them: "So, whether you eat or drink, or whatever you do, do all to the glory of God" (1 Cor. 10:31).

The end of our prayer shows how much the word of God has transformed us. It differentiates a hypocrite from a true Christian. While the hypocrite seeks his glory in things he does and says, a true believer seeks the glory of God. "Not to us, O Lord, not to us, but to thy name give glory for the sake of thy steadfast love and thy faithfulness" (Ps. 115:1). It is a dishonor to seek, desire or ask for things that do not give God glory. In his priestly prayer, Jesus recounts how the end of everything is God. "'Now my soul is troubled. And what should I say, Father, save me from this hour? No, it is for this reason that I have come to this hour. Father, glorify your name.' Then a voice came from heaven, 'I have glorified it, and I will glorify it again'" (Jn. 12:27-28). Our God is awesome, transcendent, powerful, all-knowing, and holy.

Jesus tells us that "Holy" is his name, and his essential identity is independent of whether we exist to sense its wonder or not. When we pray and say, "For the sake of Your holy Name Lord," we mean that the outcome will give God glory even though we are the beneficiaries.

This disposition is the fragrance that graces the heart of prayer. It is better appreciated when we interpret it in the context of Ezekiel (36:22-23). He prophesied that for the sake of God's name, he would call the people from diaspora and exile and restore them to their land. According to him, the divine motive for this restoration was that God might hallow his holy name. Looking at this prayer through the lens of Ezekiel's prophecy makes it a prayer about the return of God's people, but at the same time, it acknowledges that God's name is hallowed by his works. Then God's response to our prayers hallows his name for what he does for his people.

This brings us to the third disposition in Jesus' prayer: "Thy Kingdom come." Which kingdom is he talking about? It is the reign of God. It exists where the will of God prevails. When we say "thy kingdom come", we express our desire to live in his reign. Here we are disposed to pray as kingdom children and show what we mean by a life of obedience to the commandments (Jn. 14:23).

When we pray, "Thy kingdom come," we acknowledge that what we have on earth is not perfect or permanent. We acknowledge by it that the world of the human person is imperfect with uncontrollable challenges. We acknowledge that we are living in an uncertain world that is full of accidents, and that our world is unstable because of our sins and limitations. We acknowledge our longing for a "city with foundations, whose architect and builder is God" (Heb. 11:10). In this prayer then, we ask for God's intervention to supply us with our needs and grant us certainty, protection, care, courage, strength, and stability. In this way, our prayer becomes a humble acknowledgment of why Jesus came into the world: to do the will of his Father and thereby break the chains of wickedness, undo the works of sin, untie the cords of the yoke, set the oppressed free, and destroy the works of the devil (Is. 58:6; 1 Jn. 3:8). So, to pray for God's kingdom to come is to pray for the reign of God to prevail in our lives, works, and the world.

Because the kingdom of God bespeaks of his sovereignty, when we say "thy kingdom come," we acknowledge God's sovereignty in prayer. When we do, we are pulled away from our ego and transformed from within. This is how prayer transforms us. It shakes the core of our being and affects our thoughts, words, and actions. This disposition teaches us that prayer demands total surrender to the divine will, authority, and power. The one praying also acknowledges that prayer presupposes that the human person has limited powers to serve his needs and, as a dependent being, owes his life and sustenance to God. "And this is the confidence that we have toward him, that if we ask anything according to his will, he hears us. And if we know that he hears us in whatever we ask, we know that we have the requests that we have asked of him" (1 Jn. 5:14-15). So, this awareness disposes us to call upon God to help our reasoning and to see and accept the change we need to make in the face of our challenges.

In this, we demonstrate that God, who has absolute power ready to intervene in the lives of his people for their well-being, possesses everything the human person needs to enjoy the right living. By this acknowledgment, we ask that his reign in heaven be experienced here on earth by intervening in our lives, needs, and environment. Through our appeal, we tell him about our needs that we cannot provide by our own power. According to C.S. Lewis, God seems to do nothing of Himself which He can possibly delegate to His creatures. For instance, God will not do by a miracle what we can do by obedience.

Is it any wonder why Jesus teaches us to ask God for our daily bread? Yes, for Jesus the Our Father tells us something about our humanity. It tells us that we depend on God for our needs. In this sense, prayer is not merely about asking for food "from hand to mouth" but about the total care of human living. It is about the preservation of human life through food, shelter, and medicine. In this way, the use of bread becomes a metaphor for human needs. Bread refers to material things that we need to sustain our life. We are to ask for it daily because such things represented by bread are perishable. So, we demonstrate that day by day, after praying to God, we go to our job to work for the bread we eat. In so doing, Jesus teaches us that prayer is a petition made to God for things we need here and now.

On a deeper level, God, as our Father, knows more than our body language; he anticipates our needs and supplies them accordingly. "If you know how to give good food to your children, how much more will your heavenly Father" (Matt. 7:11). God knows that we live in a world of need and are limited in our ability to meet all our needs. He then sustains us in being. A good prayer takes these sentiments into consideration.

Fourthly, prayer demands an innocent disposition of the heart. "And forgive us our debts, as we also have forgiven our debtors" (Matt. 6:12). The one who prays does not only strive to be at peace with God but with neighbors. In line with this, the psalmist says, "Who may climb the mountain of the Lord? Who may stand in his holy place? Only those whose hands and hearts are pure, who do not worship idols and never tell lies" (Ps. 24:3-4). The mountain of the Lord is a reference to the place of prayer where we go before the Lord. We come to this meeting clean or prepared to confess and receive mercy. So, prayer calls for a clear conscience on the part of the intercessor. "But I say to you that if you are angry with a brother or sister, you will be liable to judgment; and if you insult a brother or sister, you will be liable to the council; and if you say, 'You fool,' you will be liable to the hell of fire" (Matt. 5:24). This is why Jesus teaches us to be free from being indebted to anyone with regard to loving our neighbor. "And forgive us our sins, for we also forgive everyone who sins against us" (Lk. 11:4). This task of forgiveness as a disposition does not come easily. It is possible by grace. Through Christian prayer, God freely gives the grace that stretches us to do things that do not come easily, namely, to forgive those who have offended us as God forgives us. This is so because prayer is transformative.

It changes us and redirects our perspectives. It provides an opportunity to reconcile with God and with our neighbor. We either go to prayer with a clear conscience or confess our weakness during prayer. In this way, prayer enriches us and brings out the best in us.

As a celebration directed to God, the Father of all people, there is no way we can feel comfortable going on asking for the love of God when we know that we do not love someone created in his image, or when we know that we have not given a good account of our stewardship, when we know that we are holding someone at ransom for a cause that should be forgiven, when we know that we are possessing something that does not belong to us, when we know that we are living in sin or taking advantage of somebody's sweat by trick. God is just and loving. He wants us to be sincere, just, and loving. He wants us to be people of goodwill.

The willingness to forgive and let go of those who have offended us to obtain God's forgiveness bespeaks a clear conscience. In this way, Jesus made prayer the plea of a sincere person to a God who cherishes innocence and sincerity. It is not an appeal from a bad will, ill luck, or ill motive but goodwill. Therefore, prayer should be said to benefit me and others for my own well-being and others. Prayer should reflect the character of God, who blesses the good and the bad alike and asks us to: "Be merciful, even as your Father is merciful" (Lk. 6:36).

Fifth, Jesus teaches his disciples the disposition of total surrender to the will of God. Because Jesus asks us to pray, we erroneously think that prayer is a magic wand. Jesus did not only teach us to ask for our daily bread but also to do so according to the will of God. In this way, prayer becomes the celebration of God's will. Christian prayer is, therefore, to be directed according to the will of God. Unfortunately, often we come to God in prayer with our own will. Even when we say we are asking according to his will, we still have our will intact. Our desire is to have our will granted. When our prayer is answered, and our request is granted, what we want, what we desire, or our concern - we say God is good and faithful. In this case, our will can be said to be at par with God's will. The problem comes when what we want differs from what God wills. At this time, if our request is not granted, we are not happy. We go on praying and looking forward to seeing it granted. And until it is granted, we feel God is delaying our requests, or may be angry with us, or he is not interested in our well-being. But we fail to know that prayer is directed to God's will, and he should be allowed to do what is best.

The failure to supply our needs does not mean God is uninterested in our well-being. It may mean that God wants something more for us to realize the answer to our prayer. This is the confidence we have in approaching God: "that if we ask anything according to his will, he hears us" (1 Jn. 5:14). At times, God wills it but does not allow it to be realized immediately. He may choose to do so to allow us to put certain things in order before realizing a request he has already willed. Sin can be the problem (Jos. 7:10-13), or lack of diligence (1 Thess. 3:10), lack of forgiveness (1 Pt. 2:1,2), or lack of perseverance (Lk. 18:1-8), lack of faith (Heb. 11:6), or a wrong motive (Jm. 4:3), or inordinate ambition and selfish pleasure (Jm. 4:3). What all this means is that our lack of proper repentance can be an obstacle to God answering our prayer. God's will may be that we repent for our request to be granted. It means that prayer calls for cooperating with the grace of God. It is not only about what we ask for in prayer but also whether what we are asking for is in line with God's will or not.

I am saying that some prayers call for personal actions to facilitate the realization of one's intentions. Personal actions can range from personal transformation to what the eyes can see, hands can do, and the mind can think. When Saul of Tarsus was converted on the road to Damascus, trembling and astonished, he said, "Lord, what do you want me to do?" (Acts 22:10). He recognized that obedience to God's will for him was to be the central focus of the rest of his life. In like manner, the one who prays is required to live a life that is pleasing to God (Rom. 12:1). It is one thing to claim to have faith and pray in faith, and another thing to be a willing vessel (2 Tim. 2:20-21) that is permissive to God's grace. Today, some Christians call on God day and night through long adoration and vigil prayers, asking him to endorse their plans and prospects. In reality, these plans involve forgery, lies, cheating, fraud, inordinate ambition, manipulations, selfishness, and the like. Sometimes prayer requests for employment, success, strength, and even spiritual gifts are not wrong, but they can become selfish prayers if they do not flow from a heart that is determined to obey God (Jm. 4:1-3).

What God may require of the Christian in his prayer may be to watch and pray for God's will for him. It is not then enough to pray in some circumstances without watching at the same time for the will of God to realize our intentions. I learned my lesson in 1998 when I was praying against repeated stealing going on in the rectory. We prayed for three months and became confused why the stealing continued and the thief could not be caught. When at last the thief was caught in the fourth month, I discovered that he could have been caught the first month of prayer but my lack of vigilance. I kept vigil and engaged friends and groups in prayer but did not keep watch. I did not read the signs around me revealed by God over and over again. The thief was presented to me physically several times, but my eyes were closed because it did not come the way and fashion I expected.

Is it any wonder why Jesus tells his disciples to watch and pray? We are not only to pray but also to watch for obstacles to prayer and remove them from our path. We are to watch for what God wants us to do to realize our intentions and heed them. We are to watch for what God wants us to do to realize our prayer intention for success, prosperity, and wellness. He may want us to learn a trade, go to school, maintain some cleanliness, shift our values, reorder our priorities, or refocus our vision. We are to watch by listening to what God says about our needs. In this case, we do not need to have the gift of vision or prophecy to listen to God in prayer. The Lord tells us that praying is not enough unless we have the right disposition.

So, it is not enough to ask God for help. When we do ask, we must be willing to do whatever we can and use whatever means God gives us. It is not enough to just say prayers. Some prayers call for more carefulness, foresight, human communication, forgiveness, patience, credibility, and innocence, for them to work. When Hezekiah heard that he would die, he prayed for a miracle, and God promised to extend his life for fifteen years. But to realize this promise, he placed a lump of figs on the troublesome boil (2 Kings 20:5-7). God did the healing but used human effort and natural means. The same is true of Naaman, the leper (2 Kings 5). He was required to do something, to bathe seven times, and God used this faith response to unleash divine healing. This reminds me of the story of the ten children walking to school one day when it suddenly dawned on them that unless they hurried, they would be late. One of them suggested that they stop and pray that they would be on time. "No," the other replied, "let us pray while we run as fast as we can." When we ask God to do something, we must also be ready *to do our own part*. As the saying goes: "We must pray as if everything depends on God, but work as if everything depends on us."

The fact of the matter is that as participants in a covenantal relationship with God, the Christian has a role to play in prayer, especially when it demands the use of potential already given to man by God. For instance, God gifted me with intelligence. It becomes my duty to take my studies seriously to make good grades. If I am lazy and depend only on prayer but fail to study, I will fail in my role to enhance my success and to pray according to God's will. The fact that I make a distinction in Examinations does not mean that I do not need God or prayer.

Instead, it means that I should pray to use my gift to meet my expectation as a person thus gifted. In other words, there is something God does in prayer and something I need to do to cooperate with his grace and will for me. When these two roles are together, whatever happens, is for the good of the child of God.

THE NECESSITY OF PRAYER

Prayer is indispensable for all who believe in God. It is the means by which we celebrate God's living presence among his people. It celebrates that God is at work in our world. As such, prayer expresses our hope and nourishes our faith in the promises of God and in the accomplishments of Jesus that he is able to deliver those who trust in him. We may not see the effects of our prayers or even of the actions of our communities to right the wrongs that we see in our time, but our faith and prayer are signs of God at work in our world and our lives.

The Old Testament is full of God's constant invitation to his servants to pray. He did so because of the important role prayer plays in human life. Similarly, prayer was a necessary preparation for every important event in the life of Jesus. Whenever Jesus entered prayer, he came out with results. Before the beginning of his public ministry, he fasted and prayed for 40 days and nights. The fruit showed itself in overcoming the devil's temptations (Matt. 4:1-11). On the Mount of Transfiguration, while he was praying, he was transfigured, and suddenly Moses and Elijah appeared. The result was the strengthening of the Apostles' faith in Jesus and hope in the reward of heaven (Matt. 17:1-8, Mk. 9:2-8, Lk. 9:28-36). Before he entered his passion at Gethsemane, he prayed and was given the strength to undergo his passion (Matt. 26:36-56).

Our human limitations call for prayer. Given our limitations and the challenges that come our way as human beings, we strive each day to pull through the vicissitudes of life by reaching out for external help. For believers in Christ, though the support of a fellow human being is of great help, our surest help comes from God. David believes this and, in the moment of need, said: "I will lift up my eyes to the mountains; from where shall my help come? My help shall come from the Lord who made heaven and earth" (Ps. 121:1-2). Is it any wonder why the Christian's response to life's problems is prayer? Instead of complaining, getting fed up, crying, or giving in to depression, we should use prayer to invite God into our situation. Jehoshaphat is a living example of inviting God into difficult moments and telling him that he has nowhere to go but come to him (2 Chron. 20:1ff). The disciples of Jesus present another example of prayer in response to a dreadful situation when faced with a storm in the sea of Galilee (Mk. 4:35ff). They called out to God and were saved. Paul and

Silas, who had every reason to blame God for their arrest after preaching the word of God, also have similar testimony of response to prayer when locked up in prison (Acts 16:25ff). As a matter of fact, our human needs call for prayer.

Jesus tells us to pray because prayer is efficacious and effective. This does not mean that God does not know what we need or would not help unless we pray. He knows and cares for our needs. We must pray to demonstrate faith in his spoken words concerning our human needs. St. Augustine says that God does not have to be told what we truly need. We need to pray, says the saint, to prepare ourselves for what God will give us. God may say yes to us, or God may say yes but not now to our request. Ordinarily, we expect God to grant exactly every request we make. But we fail to realize that no good parent gives his or her children everything they want.

Similarly, God chooses which one of our requests to grant an immediate response and which one to defer. One preacher once said that a refusal or an alternative response is just as much an answer as a yes. We must know that whenever we are trapped in our own agenda, we overlook God's answer to our prayers. Christian prayer, like the fiat of the Blessed Mary, invites us to be open to what God wills, trusting the love and mercy of God. There is a saying that when we take our life experiences to prayer, it may or may not change the outcome, but it will certainly change our perspective.

But it takes a willing spirit and foresight to realize this change of perspective.

The same is true about warfare prayer. The human person is a network of battles, both external and internal. While as believers, we seek to live under the reign of the Lordship of Jesus; we are at war with the evil powers of darkness (Eph. 6:10-20); we are engaged in the battle between God's truth and the lies of Satan that captivate and distort the minds of people (2 Cor. 10:3-5). Life experiences help to teach us that life is full of adventures, accidents, and harsh experiences. The world is not a safe place. As such, our lives are always in danger through terrorist attacks, tornados, earthquakes, political upheavals, hunger, coronavirus, and death, to mention but a few. These experiences do not just come our way because we are saints or sinners but because we are living in the world. So, while here on earth, we are paddled on every side by forces hostile to the kingdom of God.

From Jesus's teaching, we learn that prayer is a Christian's response to the world of temptation and satanic attacks. God knows that to live in the world is to be engaged in a battle of some sort. In view of this, Jesus taught his disciples to ask the Father in prayer to deliver them from the test. Through prayer, God intervenes to identify with us and defends us in the face of the enemy. By praying and trusting him, Jehoshaphat is told, "Because you have nowhere to go but to come to me, the battle is no longer your own, but the Lord's" (2 Chron. 20:15). Prayer becomes a way of transforming a situation for our own advantage. Jesus uses it to teach how this transformation can be achieved by persistent living in communion with God in faith and hope. We, too, experience a similar identification with him when we invite him into our situations through prayer. Just as he intervened and vindicated Jesus before the world, so he does for us before heaven and earth as his children. Prayer then makes present the power of God over temptations and attacks of the devil.

So, for the Christian, prayer is indispensable, not only because it should be a way of life but also because it is power packed. The power of prayer, according to Chrysostom, a 5th-century Church father, has subdued the strength of fire, bridled the rage of lions, silenced anarchy, extinguished wars, appeased the elements, expelled demons, burst the chains of death, enlarged the gates of heaven, relieved diseases, averted frauds, rescued cities from destruction, stayed the sun in its course, and arrested the progress of the thunderbolt (Quoted in Kent R. Hughes, James: Faith That Works, Illinois: Crossway, 1991, 145). In sum, prayer has the power to destroy whatever is opposed to the good. There is no one who has a practice of prayer who does not have a testimony of the efficacy and power of prayer.

In a world where relationships break with equanimity, the Christian's spirit of loving in the face of strife and hatred is awakened by prayer to make peace with our enemies. When such a situation arises, prayer, as Jesus teaches us, becomes the means that stretches us to do things that do not come easily. "Forgive us our sins for we ourselves forgive everyone in debt to us" (Lk. 11:4). The grace needed to forgive is often gained from prayer.

The Lord's prayer teaches us that the child of God is constantly recreating to maintain the beauty in which he is created. While the Lord wants us to come to him with our needs and to transform bad situations into good, our prayer can transform our hearts and minds. In other words, prayer is transformative. It is not so much about what we say but about how our interaction with the Lord impacts us. In prayer, where listening is fostered and understanding sown, mercy grows, love flourishes, peace is cultivated, and generosity is instilled. In prayer, we provide a moment of divine anointing that breaks the yoke of sin and difficult cases.

This transformative nature of prayer is witnessed by the Publican, who went to the temple to pray (Lk. 18:14). At the time of Jesus, Publicans were hated by all because they collected taxes for the pagan Roman Empire and, at times, charged more than the emperor mandated them. As such, the Publicans were generally regarded as public sinners. But standing before the presence of God in the temple, without innocence and justice to his credit, the grace of prayer disposed the Publican to see his unworthiness, admit his sins, and confess, and Jesus declared him forgiven. The secret of his forgiveness lies in the honest admission of his unworthiness that became more evident in prayer. The tax collector did recognize God as the source of all good and asked only for God's compassion and forgiveness. God's divine presence provoked his consciousness of sin and the self. His prayer earned him a new life. With the Publican, Jesus teaches us that prayer is, first and foremost, transformative. It is not simply getting things for ourselves but getting to know God - the kind of knowledge that brings about change.

Christians generally accept that prayer brings change, but what is not generally understood is how this change happens. Those who believe that prayer brings change say that the change happens in what we ask about but not about us. Often, we pray to God to ask for things that we want him to change or even pray to change God's mind. With this in mind, we measure our prayers by what happens outside of us but fail to know that the purpose of prayer is to change us, not God. An eminent Scripture scholar, Raymond Brown, once said, "If no change occurs as a result of prayer, then one has not really prayed." In other words, prayer is not a matter of changing things externally but one of working miracles in a person's inner nature. In this way, prayer becomes the continual practice of pulling along everything about the person who prays into God's presence and inviting him to bring healing and restoration to their internal brokenness.

It is important to note that God desires to empower me and you in all our weaknesses to change the world. In prayer, we invite God into our problems so that he will change us and enable us to change our situation. It rarely happens that a person in a state of sin goes before the All Holy God in prayer without being provoked to repentance. This is why it baffles me that despite much praying in my part of the world, morning and night, corruption, bribery, political rivalry, occult worship, kidnapping, hatred, and stealing are still commonplace.

The author of the book of Sirach reminds us that those who allow God to change their hearts in prayer make other discoveries. According to him, God is impartial in response to our prayers and is not swayed by social status but by authentic prayer offered and sincere service.

For him, the prayer of the humble does not rest until "it reaches its goal" (Sir. 35:17-19). God, who hears all prayers, has the power to change weeping into laughter, weakness into strength, oppression into freedom, and complaint into contentment.

Because of the vital place of prayer in living out our Christian life, Jesus taught us to pray in and out of season, and to persist in prayer. He used the parable about a widow who could not get what was due to her from a corrupt judge to teach us the need to persevere in prayer (Lk. 18:4-5). In this parable, Jesus sets out to teach us that prayer should be a needed response to troubling situations. Just as the widow encountered a problem that made her seek the judge's help, we, too, experience some daily problems that may call for help. Instead of complaining, getting fed up, or giving in to despair, God wants us to call upon him in times of trouble (Psalm 50:15), to call upon him against the storms of life (Mk. 6:34), and to ask him to deliver us from every evil (Matt. 6:13). When we go to him and ask for his intervention, we are fighting our problems with God. It is essential to know that we do not fight alone in our warfare prayer; Jesus fights with us. Jesus gives us his prayer support by interceding for us incessantly at the right hand of God (1 Pt. 3:22; Heb. 4:14). All we need do is not just to pray and become tired but to endure with trust. Our persistence reveals our undying hope and unrelenting faith in the necessity of prayer.

Persistent prayer of this kind is not riddled with activism, as some may think. Even though it looks like doing the same thing repeatedly, we expect different results in persistent prayer. A Christian's persistent prayer, repeated over again, may be seen by non-believers as insane. But for the Christian, it is rooted in the hope that is not vague, in the hope that gives certainty and courage to face the future. Hope, then, is the belief in possibilities beyond possibilities. Hope trusts that God will answer our petitions in ways and times beyond our knowing. Such hope allows us to trust in the possibilities beyond possibilities that God hears prayers, that miracles do happen, that life does not end in death, and that life is not limited to the present world but has an eternal dimension. In this way, a persistent intercessor believes the author of the book of Sirach that prayer does not rest until "it reaches its goals" (35:17-19).

Therefore, prayer affords us the opportunity to drink from a source outside ourselves.

It is a way we amass strength from outside of ourselves. While everyone is strong and energetic, we often need strength from outside of us to sustain us. While some seek it in an energy drink, others seek it in marijuana. Still, others seek it through drugs or guns. Though these external sources can give energy, their powers do not last. Prayer is another way of amassing strength and energy that last and endure for life. It helps us let God's strength do what our strength cannot do for us.

As a matter of fact, prayer is the key to great miraculous accomplishments. It is a communion between God and his children and an encounter with the divine. It is the most excellent way to release God's power in our lives. The prophets prayed. Moses' hand of prayer won a battle for Israel. Jehoshaphat's prayer of praise won a battle for Israel. The prayer of Shadrach, Meshach, and Abednego drove Nebuchadnezzar to enthrone the religion of Israel in Babylon. Daniel terrorized the bureaucrats of Babylon with his prayer. Elijah prayed, and fire fell from heaven. Jesus had a powerful prayer life. He prayed all night, and signs and wonders accompanied his teachings during the day. Believers prayed, and Peter was released from prison by an angel. Paul and Silas prayed, and anointing came down on the people, broke loose their prison chains, and released them. The indispensability of prayer is beyond human rhetoric.

Christian prayer, therefore, is the Christian way of life. In prayer, the Christian interacts and communes with God and with one another. It is real and calls for guts and faith, hope and courage, persistence, and an irresistible spirit to confront challenging situations.

To be a Christian, then, is to be prayerful, to have a prayer life. It is a common saying that a prayerless Christian is a powerless Christian. When burning wood ceases to produce heat, there is no more fire. The wood is only occupying space. The fire is gone. In the case of a believer, when there is no culture of prayer life, they become a mere figurehead. There is no spiritual energy, no spark of life. This way of being Christian is opposed to the way of the divine and the spirit, known for its animation, steam, and power of life.

So, while Christianity is not a religion of prayer but of life, prayer is an indispensable part of that life. It is a celebration of that abundant life. It is our ladder to the throne of God's presence, the path of transformation, and our amour against the attacks of the enemy. It is also the wellspring of divine blessings, a source of sanctification, a pool of cleansing and purification, an ocean of grace, an oasis of mercy, and the source of life for God's people. As a Christian, therefore, lift your hand in prayer and do not relent. Celebrate it with joy and be enlivened by it in and out of season.

Peter said to them, "Repent, and
each of you be baptized in the name
of Jesus Christ for the forgiveness
of your sins; and you will receive
the gift of the Holy Spirit.

Acts 2:38

CHAPTER 8

IT IS A Sacramental Life

*T*he Church believes and teaches that God is gracious and gives grace freely to his people. He does not only give grace but provides external means of dispensing it to his people. God has demonstrated this throughout history by various means. The most conspicuous of this was when the Word took flesh in Mary through the Spirit, and "became among us" and was born in Bethlehem. Through this, the invisible God becomes visible, and the world becomes divinized. Then through the Incarnation, God enters all enfleshed beings and invites us to see divine occasions in the circumstances of our lives. In this divine-human relationship, God proclaims that who we are as humans and how we live are important. If God is thus with us, then who we are matters, and what we do counts. In this way, life becomes a place of encounter with God. By that token, God becomes present to humans. We respond to this presence in the everyday moments and ordinary activities that make up our lives. This means that both humanity and divinity have the capacity to receive each other. The implication is that our life's adventures and experiences have divine occasions that remind us over and over again that all things happen for our good (Rom. 8:28).

To say that the world is divine means that we can now find God in everything. Creation is a work of divine art. God's presence sustains all creatures in existence. God is omnipresent, and as such, God is indwelling or immanent in all things. It is to be understood that God's immanence does not mean he is fully manifest in any creature. All created things provide a limited expression or revelation of creative power but cannot fully exhaust it. However, this understanding has nothing to do with the reality of pantheism. God's presence in creation does not mean pantheism. Pantheism is the belief that reality is identical to divinity or that God consists of everyone and everything. In fact, it means that since God is everything, everything is God. This is not true. God's omnipresence does not remove his transcendence. God as the creator of the universe, is transcendent because he is independent of the universe and surpasses all creation. This is where the New Age religion gets it wrong: it affirms divine immanence but denies divine transcendence.

So, that the world is divine is not the vague and dilute divine presence that a muddled pantheism preaches. What is meant instead is that God communicates himself to us in and through the world, natural things, and objects. It is that God can use humans, natural objects, ceremonies, words, and prayers to make his power and presence felt or make his will available. We perceive the divine in what God has made, creation itself, and we hear his voice in the Scriptures. In other words, the grace of God can be encountered in varied ways in the world through natural means. So, our human capacity for God means that we can enter, take root, and find eternal rest in him.

Though God can bring anything into being without any material or human agent, the history of God's relationship with his children teaches us that he regards communication through external signs as most appropriate to the nature of humans. There is nothing in this world God cannot put to use. He has been known to use what is familiar to us to reach us and make his presence and grace felt. Just as God reaches us through the finite, we reach God through the finite. The point at which this divine interchange occurs is the point of the sacramental encounter. In other words, Sacrament is God's way of relating to or interacting with humans.

The Bible reveals some ways God has communicated with his people in history using external signs and words. The sacramental use of the things of nature to make God's riches physically present can be seen in the staff of Moses, which he used to cause water to flow at the command of God (Ex. 20:11), or in the use of the bronze serpent in the desert to heal those bitten by snakes (Num. 21:28-29), or the goatskin mantle of Elijah which he used to transfer the power of his Spirit to Elisha (2 Kings 2:8, 14) or in the burning bush which he used to make sacramental the land on which Moses was standing (Exd. 3:2). In this we have fire and land embodying the presence of God.

We also see sacramental power revealed in Elisha's remains that were used to raise a dead man to life (2 Kings 13:21). God made the waters of the Jordan river sacramental when he used it to give healing to Naaman after washing seven times in it (2 Kings 5:14ff). The same divine presence is what we see in the laying on of hands and anointing of oil to ordain priests and prophets and impart on them the Spirit, as well as in Baptism and other laying on of hands in prayer by prophets and the apostles (1 Kings 19:16; Mk. 6:13).

In the New Testament, we see God's divine power in the Jordan water that was used to bring baptismal birth to Jesus and those born into his kingdom (Lk. 3:21-22). The same is also true in how Jesus used the mixture of sand and saliva to give sight to the blind (Jn. 9:6-7), or in how Paul used a handkerchief to heal the sick and cast out demons (Acts 19:12). In all these circumstances, God makes available his divine power and presence through material means to humanity, either by forgiving their sins, healing their sickness, feeding them, preparing them for a good death, or making available his favors to men and women in answer to their internal aspirations and prayers.

Though some of these external matters served as symbols in the Old Testament, they now embody Jesus Christ, to whom they all pointed in the Old Testament, in whom lies the meaning of them all. So, it should not be a surprise why in the age of grace, we still receive supernatural realities by natural means and sensible signs as exist in the sacraments. In these ways, the Lord continues to be present, and the sacraments are said to be channels of grace and are what the Fathers of the Church specifically referred to as Mysteries. The Latin rendering of the term "mystery" is sacramentum, a sacrament.

WHAT IS A SACRAMENT

By sacrament, we mean any matter or finite reality which embodies and communicates God's presence or power. St. Augustine calls it an "outward sign of inward grace." By this, he means that a sacrament has matter and form. While the matter of a sacrament is visible, the form is invisible. In the invisible form lies the grace that is made real and visible by matter. In this way, sacraments become a means of using material things to communicate grace to human beings through the prayer of the Church. So, sacraments are efficacious signs of grace instituted by Christ and entrusted to the Church, by which divine life is dispensed to us.

There are seven of these "channels of grace" the Church recognizes as sacraments: Baptism, Confirmation, Holy Eucharist, Reconciliation, Anointing of the Sick, Holy Orders, and Matrimony. God is embodied in each of these sacraments. As such, each one is a means of giving or receiving grace. God can put them to use to communicate his presence as each is administered to the faithful. In this way, the sacraments can be understood as the celebration of the Presence of God. For in the sacraments, God is present to baptize with the hand of the priest, to administer Confirmation with the laying on of the hands of the bishop, and to consecrate and feed believers with his Body and Blood through the action of the priest at Mass, to forgive sins with the absolution of the priest, to heal humans of sickness or prepare them for a good death with the anointing of the priest, and to join men and women in holy Matrimony through the officiation of the priest. In this way, Sacraments convey Christ's presence in all the key moments of life: birth, coming of age, marriage, hunger and sustenance, forgiveness, wellness, and death.

THE SACRAMENTAL PRESENCE OF GOD

The word "sacramental" refers to any finite reality through which blessings are received. "Sacramentals are sacred signs which bear a resemblance to the sacraments. They signify effects, particularly of a spiritual nature, which are obtained through the intercession of the Church. By them, men are disposed to receive the chief effect of the sacraments, and various occasions in life are rendered holy" (Catechism of the Catholic Church, No 1667). It is all about blessings. Every blessing praises God and prays for his gifts. Sacraments are visible signs that give invisible grace to those who worthily receive them.

The seven channels of grace are called sacraments because they are the acts of God and the acts of Christ. Through these acts, God continues to be sacramentally present with his Church, giving birth to Christian life and sustaining it. He is the principal cause of the sacraments who freely offers access to his life through grace. He alone can authoritatively give external material rites the power to confer grace to human beings. In other words, the sacraments are not caused by human forces but by God acting in and through Christ and the Church. The minister of the sacrament is only an instrumental cause of the sacrament. This means that sacraments are not wrought by the righteousness of either the celebrant or the recipient but by the power of God. However, the fruits of the sacraments depend on the disposition of the one who receives them. This is important because a sacrament is not a magic wand. It calls for a response that comes from faith and reconciliation from the recipient. When the required disposition is absent, the sacrament may be validly celebrated while it is received illicitly. But when we receive the sacraments licitly, we embody the sacramental presence of God and all the intended blessings.

God's sacramental presence can be perceived in whatever comes in contact with him. It took the coming of God in human flesh to this earth for the world to be caught up with divine presence. Though Jesus has gone to the Father, the enduring presence of Christ in creation is with us. He continues to dwell among us in specific and identifiable ways, radiating his presence throughout the world in specific and orderly forms. The point at which this divine interchange happens is the point of sacramental encounter. In other words, it is the presence of God that inheres in a matter that makes it a sacrament and a means of grace. Thus, when God intervenes in nature, it begins to embody his divine presence. As human or inanimate as matter can be, when thus inhabited, it begins to give and communicate grace.

As a result, the Church invites us to look beyond the outward signs of the sacraments and discover Jesus, who is the mediator of the new covenant and who does the action in the sacraments. It is important to note that the matter that embodies divine presence is not another God but the presence of the only one and true God. The divine presence in the sacraments does not limit or diminish the being of God as our heavenly God and Almighty Father. In fact, God is never reduced in who he is by his presence in the sacraments.

One of the arguments proposed today by non-Catholics about the sacraments is that they are not relevant in this age of grace. For them, Jesus is the fulfillment of the law (Matt. 5:17), the Old Testament signs and mysteries. Therefore, with him, there is no need for sacraments or acknowledging God's sacramental presence. He has fulfilled all of them in himself. In this way, they consider the sacraments as a human institution and something that should not exist if we truly believe in Jesus and his work of salvation. This is not true. While Jesus is the fulfillment of the law and the prophets, he is the one who instituted the sacraments. As such, sacraments are not in conflict with the Lord's work of salvation. As a matter of fact, the sacraments are an action of Jesus Christ and very essential for salvation.

The saving work of Jesus Christ is not in any way undermined by the existence of the sacraments. We all know and believe that Jesus is our Savior. "There is no other name given to us in heaven and on earth in which there is salvation but the name of Jesus Christ" (Acts 4:12).

The sacraments are not opposed to this belief and are not another means of salvation. They are the channels that enable our birth, belief, growth in God, and practice of the faith that leads to salvation in Christ. *As a matter of fact, we do not worship matter but worship the creator of matter, who became matter for the sake of his children.*

So, we perceive the divine in everything God made. Our God is sacramentally involved in the affairs of his people. This understanding helps us get over our Deism. Deism is a belief in a sort of "clock-maker" God, a god who does indeed exist but does not have much to do with his people's ongoing life. On the contrary, the God we have come to know through our Jewish and Christian experiences is present to us. He is Omnipresent and Omnibenevolent. He is our refuge and strength, a very present help in trouble (Ps. 46:1). His presence sustains all creatures in existence.

LIVING A SACRAMENTAL LIFE

Because sacraments are carriers of grace and vitality, to feed on them is to live sacramentally. Right from the day we become believers in Christ, our lives are nourished sacramentally on a daily basis. Our sacramental life reveals itself in the way we constantly avail ourselves of the sacraments. Baptism begins our life in Christ and opens the door of sacramental living. It does this by transforming the baptized from being an ordinary person created in the image of God to becoming a Christian person. With it, we begin to enjoy the privilege that belongs to the sons and daughters of God, as well as share in the dignity that belongs to the Holy Trinity. We become privileged members of the family of God with the right to eternal life.

Through Baptism, we are born again, become God's children, and begin to share in the life of grace. This is so because when Jesus, who knew no sin, was made to be sin on our behalf, he made us through Baptism to become the righteousness of God in him through his perfect righteousness (2 Cor. 5:21). As Jesus became part of the righteousness of humanity to live its life, through Baptism we become part of his own righteousness to live his life. By the grace of this gift, we begin to *share in eternal life through the life of grace.* The eternal life we enjoy now through grace assures us of the eternal bliss waiting for us at the end of life.

Baptism is not just an encounter that could be made and lost and repeated but an indelible sharing in the life of God. As such, the baptized live sacramentally daily as they profess faith in Christ by word and deed. A guideline from our Catechism states: "Having become a member of the Church, the person baptized belongs no longer to himself, but to him who died and rose for us. From now on, he is called to be subject to others, to serve them in the communion of the Church, and to 'obey and submit' to the Church's leaders" (CCC. 1269). So, Baptism transforms the believer into a Christian person, a sharer in divine grace, and a witness to Christ by word and deed. As such, we do not only remind ourselves about our Baptism by signing ourselves with holy water whenever we enter the house of God, but we do so anytime we avail ourselves of the works of grace. It takes constant remaining in belief and faith in God alone to live out our Baptism.

In the sacrament of Confirmation, we are infused with new life and more grace through the Holy Spirit, who seals us with the security of the Father. In this sacramental encounter, the Spirit of God, who has seized the believer's life, begins to animate him with spiritual energy. The life which the Holy Spirit produces in us makes us a "new creation" in Jesus Christ (2 Corinthians 5:17). We are given the fire of the Holy Spirit not only to purify our hearts and minds but to transform our lives into living torches of his saving love and mercy.

Confirmation makes this life in the Spirit possible by conferring the gifts of the Holy Spirit on us to strengthen our relationship with Christ. These gifts deepen our baptismal life, calling us to be missionary witnesses of Jesus Christ to the world. The gift of wisdom enables us to see the world from God's viewpoint, grasp God's purpose and plan for our lives. The gift of knowledge disposes us to see the circumstances of our lives as God sees them, to discern easily and effectively between the impulses of temptation and the inspiration of the Spirit in the light of faith. The gift of understanding allows us to grasp, in a limited way, the very essence of the truth of faith and stimulates us to work on knowing ourselves as part of our growth in knowing God. As St. Augustine puts it, "That I may know You, may I know myself?" The gift of fortitude or courage enables us to trust that God holds our future, and as such, we can face tomorrow without fear and stand up for Christ when challenged.

With the gift of counsel or right judgment, the Holy Spirit teaches the heart about moral life and trains our conscience, and in an instant, enlightens a person on what to do. The gift of piety or reverence produces an instinctive filial affection for God, a generous love toward him, and affectionate obedience that wants to do what he commands and love the one who commands it. The gift of fear of the Lord or wonder and awe in God's presence infuses honesty into our relationship with God and imparts an attitude of gratitude that God loves us and that we can share in his life. In these and other ways, the Holy Spirit continues to transform and animate our Christian life sacramentally.

When we are responsive to the grace of Confirmation and the seven gifts of the Holy Spirit, we begin to bear the fruits of the Spirit: love, joy, peace, patience, kindness, goodness, generosity, gentleness, faithfulness, modesty, self-control, and chastity (Gal. 5:22).

Through these operative channels of the gifts of the Spirit in the life of the confirmandi, the grace received at Baptism is deepened and strengthened to live sacramentally daily.

Thus bequeathed, the confirmandi joyfully takes responsibility for their own faith, makes a firm, lifelong commitment to Jesus, and is strongly connected to the community of believers, the Church. With the grace of the Holy Spirit, the confirmandi is willing to testify about his faith, share his beliefs with others, speak openly with great conviction about Jesus Christ and his Gospel, and do everything in his care to make the name of Jesus known and loved. Then living and walking by the Spirit as a lifestyle, the confirmandi lives a sacramental life. So, the Spirit is not just received and then stifled but constantly is fanned into flame through prayer, good works, and witnessing.

The sacrament of the Eucharist teaches us that life is a gift from God that needs nourishment. To do so, man occupies himself daily searching for food, water, shelter, medicine, and guidance to satisfy his hunger and preserve his life. But it takes more than material food to satisfy his hunger. Hence during his earthly ministry, Jesus presented himself as the Bread of Life that could satisfy human hunger. To do this, he created a sacrament of himself to provide divine nourishment that material food cannot give.

At the last supper, "Jesus took bread, and when he had given thanks, he broke it and gave it to his disciples, saying, "This is my body, which is given for you. Do this in remembrance of me." And likewise, the cup after they had eaten, saying, "This cup that is poured out for you is the new covenant in my blood" (Lk. 22:19-20). In this way, he gave himself to his disciples, his Body and Blood, under the form of bread and wine. In so doing, he tells us that he can be present in external substances like bread and wine to sustain human life. In this self-offering, he united the Eucharistic transubstantiation with his bloody sacrifice on the cross, thus giving it the character of sacrifice equal in value to that of the cross. This institution created a divine presence for believers to boost abundant life.

As the Bread of Life, Jesus provides a life of sacramental union with himself. "Whoever eats my flesh and drinks my blood remains in me and I in him" (Jn. 6:56). In this way, our relationship with the Lord is not only deepened but nourished. The sacramental Body and Blood of Jesus become a visible sign and an effective means of him being present to us and us being present to him. As he puts it in another place: "He who eats my flesh and drinks my blood abides in me, and I in him" (Jn. 6:51,56). It takes this interconnectivity between us and the divine to bear fruit and be sustained in being. "Just as the living Father sent me and I have life because of the Father, so also the one who feeds on me will have life because of me" (Jn. 6:57). In other words, with the Bread of Life, a life-giving relationship is established and sustained by a stream of nourishment.

So, in this sacrament, we encounter Christ's Presence. While other sacraments embody Jesus's presence and provoke an encounter with God in a sacramental manner, the Eucharist is the Real Presence of Christ. The Gospel of John tells us that Jesus is truly present when he says: "For my flesh is real food, and my Blood is true drink" (Jn. 6:55). Here, Jesus is talking about something concrete, something real, and something true. So, as difficult as it is to understand, the Eucharist is not a symbol of Christ but the real presence of Christ. It is the sacramental body and blood, soul, and divinity of Jesus. "And the bread which I shall give for the life of the world is my flesh" (Jn. 6:51). In other words, we do not receive bread; we receive Jesus.

In this offering of his flesh to eat and blood to drink, Jesus invites us to take his life into the very center of our being (Jn. 6:53). This life that he offers is the very life of God himself. It is a divine life; it is sacramental, real, and a bond of love and nourishment. So, the sacramental body and blood of Christ is a life-giving, life-sustaining, and life-nourishing sacrament. Hence, Jesus said, "Very truly, I tell you, unless you eat the flesh of the Son of Man and drink his blood, you have no life in you. Those who eat my flesh and drink my blood have eternal life, and I will raise them on the last day" (6:53-54). Through participation in this sacrament, believers continue to share in the abundant life of God (Jn. 10:10), and their lives are nourished and sustained.

As a life-giving sacrament, through the mystery of the Bread of Life, a sacramental encounter occurs, and recipients participate in eternal life. "I am the living bread that came down from heaven; whoever eats this bread will live forever; and the bread that I will give is my flesh for the life of the world" (Jn. 6:51). In the Eucharist, Jesus offers us the abundant supernatural life of heaven itself, the new manna, to sustain our spiritual lives just like the manna in the Old Testament sustained the Israelites' physical lives on their journey from Egypt to the Promised Land. He offers himself as a living Bread to feed that part of us that will never die.

In other words, the Bread of Life will save believers from spiritual death. In this regard, Jesus tells his disciples that the one who partakes of it has eternal life (Jn. 6:54) and will be raised on the last day (Jn. 6:40).

As a life-nourishing sacrament, the Eucharist feeds us for the often difficult journey of daily life. It strengthens us to live as faithful Christians in our troubled world and connects us to Jesus, the source of all spiritual strength and holiness. In other words, it helps connect us to the source of life and helps us sustain the life of grace within us, which we receive at Baptism and guides our way to heaven. Simply put, the Bread of Life is food for our journey home, food that helps us survive this world's hostile desert and arrive safely at our heavenly homeland. In fact, the sacrament of the Body and Blood of Christ provides an opportunity to live sacramentally daily by all who receive him in daily Mass.

Because receiving the Eucharist is an encounter with Jesus, living and alive, when we approach the table of the Lord, we expect to receive healing, pardon, comfort, and refreshment for our souls. When we receive from the Lord's table, we unite ourselves intimately to Jesus Christ, who makes us sharers in his body and blood. As bodily nourishment restores lost strength, so the Eucharist restores lost spiritual strength and charity and keeps us firmly rooted in the love of Christ in a sacramental relationship. "For as often as you eat this bread and drink the cup, you proclaim the Lord's death until he comes" (1 Cor. 11:26).

The mystery of our sacramental living is that it does not have one source. When a person is born again through Baptism, he or she begins a new life of grace. But when growing up, he or she does not remain in that state of grace forever. Even though we are baptized and live in the time of grace, we may not all realize the fullness of its impact on our lives every time. This new life can be weakened and even lost by sin. As we endeavor to do the will of God in a world infested with evils and temptations, our moral weakness still shows itself in our self-seeking, self-will, self-directed motives, and intentions. In fact, the moment we lose sight of God, darkness invades our lives, we miss our steps and fall, and we lose fellowship with God. As a matter of fact, the Christian life is like riding a bicycle: the moment you stop cycling the pedals, you stop moving. In like manner, when we stop starving our sinful desires, mortifying the deeds of the flesh (Rom. 8:13; Col 3:5' Gal 5:24), and exercising discipline on our cravings, we stop loving God faithfully and making progress in our faith.

But when we fail to realize this impact of being human in our Christian lives, we go on basking in the euphoria of God's love and feel that once born again, we will always live in grace. To this effect, Paul says, "Do you not know that God's kindness is an invitation to you to repent?" (Rom. 2:4). As a perfect healer, Jesus provided a sacrament for our healing with the sacrament of reconciliation. When Jesus paid for our sins on the Cross of Calvary, he established the sacrament of reconciliation to take care of the future life of the disciples. With the sacrament of reconciliation, Jesus forgives us our sins committed after Baptism through our repentance and confession (Matt. 18:18). "Those who approach the sacrament of Penance obtain pardon from God's mercy for the offenses committed against him, and are, at the same time, reconciled with the Church which they have wounded by their sins and which by charity, by example, and by prayer labors for their conversion" (CCC. 1422). By the priest's sacramental absolution God grants the penitent "pardon and peace" and imparts to the sinner the love of God who reconciles. Without this means of forgiveness, no one can live an authentic

Christian life. As often as we avail ourselves of the sacrament of reconciliation and its effects, we live sacramentally.

It is important to know that the power of the flesh weighs down on all of us with divergent appetites that provoke the desire for sin. To live a good Christian life, we need daily dying to sin, which Jesus recommends to his disciples when he tells them to deny themselves and "carry their cross and follow him" daily (Lk. 9:23-25). This calls for daily mortification and daily dying to sinful appetites and desires. Because sin needs to be dealt with and not suppressed, repentance and penance are the two weapons we can use to break with its root and begin to desire the things that make for good Christian and sacramental living.

In the sacrament of reconciliation, the Church teaches us to see our sins as "opposition" to God, who loves us so much. If we see it as an obligation, we confess our sins as a moral wrong instead of a breach of love for God. It takes love to make us see our sin as an offense against a person, the person of God. As a result, God does not want us to come to him with a prepared speech and a list of sins that do not come from conversion and repentance. Therefore, this sacrament is not concerned with the list of sins to be confessed, but a contrite heart and a broken spirit (Ps. 51:17). What Jesus demanded from Peter when he denied him is what He wants from us when we commit sin (Jn. 21:15-17). He asked Peter: "Do you love me more than these?" By this, he means: "Do you love me in such a manner as to sacrifice your life for me?" The Good News Jesus wants Peter to realize is that sin is a breach of love and communion. If Peter loves Jesus and takes his relationship with him seriously, he will never deny him again. Peter tells us that some of us can deny the Lord when our life, future, or well-being is at stake. Peter's example invites us to bring this negative side of us to God for healing. A response of this kind is how change comes, and it is much more effective and personal. In fact, forgiveness is real and therapeutic. When sins are forgiven, communion and sacramental living are restored. In this way, the sacrament of reconciliation offers incessant opportunities to live a sacramental life. In it, we celebrate that God restores what was lost, heals whatever is broken in our choices against God's holy will, and the believer begins to live again sacramentally.

On another note, living in a world where our body, mind, and emotions experience daily wear and tear due to stress, anxiety, disease, and sickness; our lives need emotional and physical healing. Therefore, knowing fully well that the infirm are in great need of healing either of soul or body, Jesus makes the sacrament of anointing an essential remedy to provide healing to the sick, to restore one's life to wellness, and for the dying to prepare for a good death when physical life is not meant to be. Through his passion, Jesus willingly entered the pains and sufferings of humanity and sacramentalized it as a means by which we can receive grace. In this sacrament, we celebrate how the crucified Lord lives today in each of us, and in our suffering, suffers with us, and in our death, dies with us and lives on in glory with us. Christ's death and resurrection give us the courage to know that love and grace accompany us on our journey to life's final victory.

So, the sacrament of anointing confers an increase of sanctifying grace on the sick and presupposes that the recipient is free from mortal sin. This is part of the reason why it is best when the sacrament of reconciliation is given before anointing. This not only opens the door of healing but also gives the grace that quiets anxiety, dissipates fear, and enables the sick person to embrace God's will and face the possibility of death with inspiring confidence in God and resignation to his will. Because the sacrament of reconciliation often precedes it and concludes with the reception of the Eucharist, it avails the recipient an opportunity to live sacramentally and have a renewed encounter with God.

It is a serious mistake to wait too long to call a priest to anoint a sick person until the advanced stages of a disease. Anointing is a vehicle of divine power for healing. The fitting time for anointing is when the sick person is still able to talk and not when in a coma. It is the sacrament for the living and not for the dead. In an emergency, call a priest to come to your home or ask for a Catholic priest at the hospital.

The Church does not prepare us only for a good life but also for love and relationship through the sacrament of Matrimony. A new kind of life emerges when a man unites himself with a woman in marriage. It is the sacrament by which a baptized man and a baptized woman bind themselves for life in a lawful marriage and receive the grace to fulfill the duties of the married state. Through the transformation of indissoluble union, the priest assists husband and wife to receive the grace of conjugal love to live for each other and to produce their kind through childbearing. This voluntary giving of each other in love gives the grace needed by husband and wife to live together validly and licitly with rights to conjugal love. As it were, relationship is sweet but not easy. Hence Paul likens marriage to the relationship between Christ and his Church. Then, seen and understood from this angle of sacrifice for the good of the other, husband and wife strive to make present the sacramental love of Jesus for his Church in their relationship. It takes grace to grapple with the challenges of marriage. Matrimony provides this grace, and when married couples dispose themselves to it and remain faithful to the vows they exchanged with each other, they live sacramentally.

The last of the seven channels of receiving grace is the sacrament of Holy Orders which is conferred by ordination to the priesthood. Jesus instituted the sacrament at the Last Supper when he gave his Apostles the power and the duty to celebrate Mass and commanded them: "Do this in remembrance of me" (Lk. 22:19). By ordination, God imparts the power of his Son's mission of dispensation of grace to the priest. Thus, the recipient of this sacrament receives power and grace to perform the sacred duties of bishops or priests. This sacrament carries a sacramental character which seals the receiver of the sacrament and consecrates him for a specific purpose within God's plan. The sacrament of Holy Orders has three degrees: the episcopate, the presbyterate, and the diaconate. The episcopate and presbyterate refer to the position of Bishop and Priest. Both of them participate in the priesthood of Christ. The Church intends the deacon to help and serve the episcopate and presbyterate. Hence the ministries conferred by ordination to the episcopate and presbyterate are conferred only on men who are ready to embrace celibacy freely and who publicly manifest their intention of staying celibate for the love of God's kingdom and the service of humanity (Matt. 19:4-6).

Like Baptism and Confirmation, ordination imprints an "indelible sacramental character" on the ordained that cannot be repeated or conferred temporarily. In this way, the priest is anointed by the Holy Spirit, who enables him to act in the person of Christ, the head. This means that within the context of the priest's service to the Church, it is Christ himself who is present as the Church's head through the action of the priest. In this way, the priest becomes an "icon" of Christ through whom divine grace and action flow. While being faithful to vows of Holy Orders makes the recipient live sacramentally, his celebrating and participating in other sacraments increases the priest's daily participation in the life of grace.

In the daily exercise of this sacrament by the priest as one configured to Christ, he does not only live for God in the practice of his gifts but makes available the sacraments to maintain the life and communion of the Church and her members. It is a sacrament that is in daily demand as priests occupy themselves with sanctifying the day and night and the people and their works through prayer and various sacramental activities. Therefore, free from many of the cares of this life, recipients of this sacrament voluntarily dedicate the energy they would otherwise spend on family life to their spiritual well-being and that of the people of God they serve. The priest does not only live sacramentally on a daily basis. However, he provides the people of God the means to live sacramentally daily through the celebration of the Mass and other sacraments.

CONCLUSION

So, the sacraments teach us that God is real and interacts with humanity in concrete manners. He is present to us and can enter our lives. Through the sacrament of Baptism God enters the life of a believer who is "born again" to live the life of grace. In Confirmation he enters the believer's life and gives him the power to live out the fruit of the Spirit: love, joy, peace, patience, kindness, goodness, faithfulness, gentleness, and self-control to serve him and humanity. In the Eucharist he enters and nourishes our life with his body and blood for us to live in him and he in us. In the sacrament of reconciliation, he enters our life to heal us from the effects of sin and orders our life on the right path. In the sacrament of anointing, he enters our pain and sacramentalizes our suffering to become a means of grace. In the sacrament of Matrimony and Holy Orders, he seals us to himself in an intimate relationship. He disposes us to serve the needs of those we are called to love in a selfless manner, either as priests or married couples.

As we can see, the Christian life is born by sacrament and nourished by sacrament. In other words, it takes the sacraments to begin the Christian life and to live a life of grace or sacramental life. Sacraments do not only make the Christian but sustain him or her because they are means of dispensing grace. It is then a joy to know that our life of grace resonates around the sacraments, which are interconnected in turn.

As Christians, therefore, we are called to live sacramentally by striving to make our lives holy and to see our work as a ministry for the glory of God. Our whole life and experience are to be given up to become one with the sacraments by which God gives his grace to us. This is important because when we live sacramentally, we become present to what is always there, that which is waiting for us to wake up and behold his presence, the invisible God who is present in things around us. In fact, when we live this way, everything becomes a means to take us to deeper truths, to the ever-present God who walks everywhere in everything.

So, it is not enough to just receive the sacraments, but we must allow ourselves to be sacramentalized by what is received. This is important because the purpose of every sacrament is to give life and communicate love. But if that love is not present in our lives, our lives become empty and hollow. In that emptiness, the sacramental living to which we are called becomes difficult to achieve. Therefore, sacramental life is about life informed by the sacraments.

It is a life of celebrating and embodying the presence of Christ in specific forms by which his grace is made available to us. It is a life animated by the presence of God, filled with love and joy, enriched by grace, and secured for all eternity. It is a way of letting who we are and what we do be done in God, with God, and through God to the glory of God.

You make known to me the path
of life; in your presence there
is fullness of joy; at your right
hand are pleasures forevermore.

Psalm 16:11

CHAPTER 9

IT IS A LIFE OF
JOY

oy is a pleasurable feeling that is characterized by human elation, delight, cheerfulness, or harmony. It is not a mere feeling of the body but a state of mind and an orientation of the heart. It is an effusive emotional response to goodness, well-being, good fortune, luck, or success. Joy can be brought about by good circumstances of what is right and just, beneficial and entertaining. In other words, joy arises from the good things that happen to us or around us. This may arise from lively interpersonal connections and networks of friendship, religious experience, and success, or experiences of loving and being loved. It may be a feeling that springs up inside us when we perceive something that has happened to us or someone we care for and love. It may result from any good news that brings pleasurable feelings. Joy is always about something, either perceived or actual. When good things thus grace our life, we perceive it as a blessing and are grateful. The fruit of our heart's gratefulness is joy.

Joy is constant, limitless, and abiding. It is not a momentary euphoric feeling that comes and goes. By its nature, joy cannot be forced on a person and, when presumed, does not last because it cannot be faked for a long time. A person must be mentally or physically engaged in something to feel a surge of graciousness within and for there to be joy. In this way, joy is not a feeling of pleasure from a sense of appetite. We do not speak of joy except when delight follows reason. It is rooted in the heart and mind, glows and beams delightfully on the face, and is expressive in words. As such, joy is a core human experience. It is a way of being and living.

Joy is not the same as happiness, but it is not devoid of it. Both joy and happiness give a good mood and come from a good turn of events. The experience of fortune, luck, success, or strength can give rise to a deep sense of gratitude and lead to happiness and joy. So, joy and happiness can be present simultaneously in a person. This is why it is sometimes difficult to guess which one is present in some people at a point in time. However, joy can be present even during unhappy times. This is because happiness is based on external stimuli. It can be momentary as it is often the result of short-term contentment. On the other hand, joy is based on internal well-being or the anticipation of well-being. It is more profound than happiness, touching the heart and spirit and long-lasting. Happiness may be affected by circumstances, but joy is independent of current circumstances in a person.

Often joy and happiness are used interchangeably. For instance, Nigerians are widely known as happy people. While this is true about Nigerians, what is at work is a combination of happiness and joy. If we consider happiness as a reality occasioned by good circumstances and well-being, Nigerians will not be near recognition in the world. The situation of things in it is not the kind that can provoke that magnitude of what is perceived to be happiness except the joy of the Lord. Nigerians are joyful people because religion characterizes everything they do. They see God in every life experience. They sing, dance and laugh when they are full or hungry, rich or poor. The Lord is their all and in all – a belief that keeps them positive and joyful in all situations. This state of living is the reason for their joy, even when social media perceive it as happiness. Despite the general collapse of their economy, justice, security, social amenities, and job, the people can never stop believing and singing the praise of God and beaming with joy.

Gladness, a synonym for joy, describes the joyous disposition of believers who give their lives and work to the service of God. David says that such believers "serve the Lord with gladness, and come into his presence with singing" (Ps. 100:2). What it means is that goodness and faith can cause joy. However, joy is not a virtue because it is not found among theological, moral, or intellectual virtues. Instead, it is the fruit of the Spirit.

DIVINE JOY

As an enduring state of being, joy has a divine undertone. It is motivated by God, whose kingdom is but love and joy in the Holy Spirit. It is the infallible sign of the presence of God within and an internal feeling of the manifestation of the Spirit. In other words, joy is occasioned by the Lord. It is one of the fruits of the action of the Holy Spirit in our soul when we identify ourselves with the Lord. As the psalmist puts it: [God] "You have put gladness in my heart more than they have when their grain and wine abound" (Ps. 4:7). While the abundance of the good things of the earth leads to gladness, there is an experience of gladness, a joy that comes from God and exceeds that which is granted by the physical world. This makes the psalmist further say that in God's presence, there is fullness of joy (Ps. 16:11) and that he makes us glad about the joy of his presence (Ps. 21:6). It is God who brings about the rejoicing and gladness. Who God is and what he does provokes joy and rejoicing. This is why joy is ignited in the believer whenever God is encountered. There is no one who truly encounters the Lord that lacks joy.

The Old Testament has lists of various things that can cause joy. We see instances of joy in the lives of the Israelites when God delivered them from bondage and suffering. Exile is one of the awful things that happened to the Israelites in biblical history, which defines the community's relationship with God. It was in 587 B.C. when Jerusalem fell to Babylon, and the nation went into exile. Plagued with so many problems, the Jews became tired of waiting during their exile for the coming of the Messiah and gave in to spiritual inactivity and fear. God told them through Isaiah never to give in to despondency because the imminent coming of the Messiah would bring positive changes that could make the redeemed of the Lord break into singing and gladness. When God finally delivered them, the lyrics of sad laments gave way to songs of joy as the people returned to Jerusalem, singing praises to God, who ransomed them from exile.

In his description of the joy of the people, the prophet Zephaniah prophesied that the day on which God restores "the remnant of Israel," removing the judgments passed against it, Israel will rejoice, and the Lord himself "will exult over you with joy" and "rejoice over you with loud singing" (Zeph. 3:16-17). According to this text, it is not only the people who rejoiced; God who wrought the miracle rejoiced that he did. He rejoiced over the wholeness and liberation of his people. It means God joins in rejoicing with his children. When joy on earth provokes heavenly joy, joy happens because heaven and earth have met and come together. Nehemiah also sees God as causing this joy, replacing grief with joy, and asks the people not to grieve, for the joy of the Lord is their strength. He further admonishes the people to go and enjoy choice food and sweet drinks and send some to those who have nothing prepared (8:10).

In these texts, joy may be the aftermath of suffering and pain. The psalmist, known for his many invitations to joy, delight, and rejoicing, also testifies that joy can be the fruit of suffering. He said, "Those who sow with tears will reap with songs of joy. Those who go out weeping, carrying seed to sow, will return with songs of joy, carrying sheaves with them (126:5-6). Joy may be "the prospect of the righteous" (Prov. 10:28), the effect of the saving power of the word of God (Jer. 15:16), or occasioned by God's deliverance (Ps. 71:23), or the effects of confidence and trust in God, and what he does as expressed by Habakkuk: "Though the fig tree does not bud and there are no grapes on the vines, though the olive crop fails and the fields produce no food, though there are no sheep in pen and no cattle in the stalls, yet I will rejoice in the Lord, I will be joyful in God my Savior" (3:17-18). In other words, to experience God is to know joy because joy is of the Lord. In an encounter of this kind, joy may come from a fulfilled promise, divine intervention, conversion, or salvation.

As we can see, the Old Testament is full of instances of joy induced by a relationship with God, by his deliverance and salvation, by victory over their enemies, by a good harvest or response to the good news of divine favors granted by God to his people. In fact, joy is not only the natural human delight in times of healing and reconciliation but also the joy of discovering that Israel's God is, at last, doing the things he has promised, rescuing the people from their "exile," and providing forgiveness, restoration, and new life.

Joy is also seen across the whole range of the New Testament: from the angelic joy to be shared with all people at the birth of Jesus (Lk. 2:10-11) through the joy when the final kingdom is revealed (Rev. 19:6-7). Here we see the joy in the Magnificat of Mary when she received the good news of her divine pregnancy and declared, "My soul magnifies the Lord, and my spirit rejoices in God my Savior" (Lk. 1:47). In other passages are the joy of repentance represented by the joy of finding a lost sheep and a lost coin (Lk. 15:1-10), the joy of the resurrection that will replace grief (16:22), the joy of the news of conversion (Acts 15:3), joy that everything happens for good to believers (Rom. 8:28), and the spirit-filled joy (Gal. 5:22-23). Some of the passages here present the appropriateness of joyful celebration resulting from the good things that have happened, namely, the repentance of a sinner, the Lord's abiding with his children, mercy, and salvation. The emphasis in these texts is that joy is of the Lord. It is the fruit of confident abiding in the goodness of the Lord. It is a feeling that comes from the assurance that God's goodness is unshakable and abides forever. Joy, in this manner, arises from knowing, believing, and experiencing a feeling that God is in control of our lives and circumstances. Because we are safe and in good hands, our joy knows no bounds.

What makes Christian joy unique is that it is produced in the believer by the Holy Spirit; it is not from mere feeling but only possible as the fruit of the Holy Spirit (Gal. 5:22). The Holy Spirit produces it as he floods our hearts with divine animation. We can say that to have the Holy Spirit is to have joy. But that is only sometimes true. There are believers who have no joy even though they have the Holy Spirit. When it is not, something is wrong. We may need to fan the Spirit into flame or search for the obstacles that make realization difficult and remove them.

As a divinely orchestrated state of being, the joy from the Spirit conveys great energy that makes the believer strong. The prophet Nehemiah knows about this divine strength. When he recalls how the redeeming power of the Lord has filled the camp of the Israelites with joy, he says: "The joy of the Lord is your strength" (Neh. 8:10). Yes, the joy of the Lord gives strength to be aglow in the spirit when overtaken by misfortune. It gives strength to withstand danger and sickness, hold on to faith, and be optimistic in the face of suffering. The joy of the Lord gives strength to the wearied, the despondent, to the one who looks up to the Lord for comfort. It gives strength in these circumstances when we allow our life of faith to help us pull through difficult times with smiles on our faces. The strength comes from believing in the ever-present presence of God in season and out of season.

JOY IN SUFFERING

The suffering of Jesus opened the door to how believers do not only endure suffering but allow the result to provoke joy. It is not natural to feel good in suffering, but Christianity defies it. It teaches us that how we respond to problems is responsible for the presence or absence of joy during difficult times. Suffering, by its nature, is painful and threatening. Human nature abhors pain and suffering. It is then not common to think of joy during hard times. While going through it is torture, and no one likes it, there are times we have the strength to put up with it because of the joy that comes from it.

We can trace this kind of joy to the time the Israelites were delivered from the agony of exile. The people were irking out their existence during their exile's long and dark times. The pain and the agony of their exile were relieved, and they were taken over by joy. This kind of joy does not accompany suffering but comes at the end of suffering. Referring to the joy that was felt when God delivered the Israelites from exile from Babylon, David said:

> *When the Lord restored the fortunes of Zion,*
> *we were like those who dream.*
> *Then our mouth was filled with laughter,*
> *and our tongue with shouts of joy;*
> *then they said among the nations,*
> *"The Lord has done great things for them."*
> *The Lord has done great things for us; we are glad.*
> *May those who sow in tears reap with shouts of joy!*
> *He that goes forth weeping, bearing the seed for sowing,*
> *shall come home with shouts of joy,*
> *bringing his sheaves with him*
>
> Psalm 126:5-6

Psalm 126 is a song that looks back to when the captives returned to Jerusalem following their seventy years of exile in Babylon. They had suffered so much, and now they suddenly found themselves back in their homeland, the city of Jerusalem. God turned their tears into joy and their sorrows into laughter when he delivered them. The lyrics of sad laments gave way to songs of joy as the people returned to Jerusalem, singing praises to God, who ransomed them from exile. It is joy purified by suffering. It is obvious that when motivated by faith, we look beyond the immediate suffering and submit ourselves to calm. According to Pope Francis, to have calm and peace in times of suffering is to have the seed of joy that will come later. It is the joy of hope. Though we may not feel it at times, it is real and does come later. Difficult times have an end; troubles do cease. Joy comes at last.

Similar to this is the joy mothers experience after the pain of delivering their babies. "When a woman is in travail, she has sorrow because her hour has come; but when she is delivered of the child, she no longer remembers the anguish, for joy that a child is born into the world" (Jn. 16:21). It's true, a woman suffers a lot in childbirth, but then when she holds her child, she forgets her pain. What remains is "the joy of a newborn baby, purified by suffering. This joy is hidden; it can only be seen with the eyes of faith that morning will come after night and that sweet accompanies sweat and crown a cross.

In addition to this teaching is Jesus' own life experience. Jesus gives us an example of enduring suffering because of the joy that will come from it. Jesus endured the cross because of the joy that would come from it. In imitation of him, some Christians have gone through martyr's death with confidence and assurance motivated by Jesus. Christians who resign their faith to God during difficult times draw strength from the example of Christ's suffering and joy from his victory.

As the letter to the Hebrews put it: "Looking unto Jesus, the author and finisher of our faith, who for the joy that was set before Him endured the cross, despising the shame, and has sat down at the right hand of the throne of God" (12:2). In this lies how the joy of the Lord gives strength to believers to bear their daily crosses with cheerful faces. Peter consolidated this when he said: "But rejoice insofar as you are sharing Christ's sufferings, so that you may also be glad and shout for joy when his glory is revealed" (1 Pt. 4:13). Is it any wonder James says: "My brethren, *count it all joy* when you fall into various trials, knowing that the testing of your faith produces patience. But let patience have its perfect work, that you may be perfect and complete, lacking nothing" (1:2-4). James tells us to be consistently calm and confident through our trials because the Lord is our strength. "For the kingdom of God is not eating and drinking, but righteousness and peace and joy in the Holy Spirit" (Rom. 14:17).

Paul is a living example of the strength of the joy of the Lord in difficult times. While imprisoned and uncertain about the outcome of his imprisonment and whether he would live or die, Paul writes that even if he is "being poured out as a libation," he remains glad and rejoices and calls on the Philippians to rejoice with him (2:17-18). Paul's joy prevailed despite the circumstances of his imprisonment and affliction. His faith that he is sharing in the sufferings of Christ, his Master, is his motivation. He sees beyond his suffering to the victory of Jesus, the Savior. In this way, joy becomes the response of the believer who presses on toward the prize, forgetting what lies behind and straining forward to what lies ahead, the heavenly call of God in Christ Jesus (3:13-14).

It is true that the work of salvation has been accomplished and the joy of freedom made open. There are still certain things in our lives, families, and nation that disfigure the presence of salvation, stifle our joy, block our vision, becloud our hope, and instill fear into our lives. We need the good news of an improved economy, the eradication of bribery and corruption, the availability of jobs, water and electricity supply, safety, and protection from kidnappers. There is no gain in saying that we live in the darkness of sin, worry, hunger, and fear. But, if we give in to the negative effects of the evils of our time and its governance, we will see no reason for joy, but if we look beyond our difficulties, we will see love and signs of love to cheer us up.

So, amid the challenges of the day, are good and positive things happening. It is the ability to see beyond the ugly side of life that opens the door to joy. It is in recognizing and celebrating in anticipation of the good ahead that we live in joy. Indeed, the reign of God may not yet be shining with the glory and splendor that we long for in our lives; Isaiah tells us that no situation in life is barren. "Sing, O barren one, who did not bear; break forth into singing and cry aloud, you who have not been in travail! For the children of the desolate one will be more than the children of her that is married, says the Lord" (54:1). With God, what appears to be a desert-like experience in our lives may turn out to be hidden fields of flowers. No matter how deep we have fallen, God is prepared to raise us. No matter how dry our life's desert is, God can make it into a green field. All we need to do is renew our trust in his unfailing promises and let go of ourselves and our activities despite the odds. Let us heed James' exhortation to wait with joyful patience because the growth of God's kingdom takes time. Though the presence of sin and suffering in our lives and society greatly affect the growth of God's kingdom on earth, God's grace transforms us and our works and disposes us to joy. So, we are able to "rejoice always" (1 Thes. 5:16) despite the many sorrowful circumstances of our lives. This is because we are not only in sorrow, pain, trouble, and suffering but also in the Lord.

Today, the Lord is still with us in our life's challenges giving us reason for joy. It takes the love of God made manifest in his Son, Jesus Christ, to feel how he is with us, calming our fears. Jesus is our Good News and the Answer to every problem. It is no longer the Angel reassuring us to "fear not" but Jesus who is with us. In fact, "fear not" has been Jesus' way of reassuring believers of his presence and company. The disciples heard it whenever they were troubled, cast down, or afraid. When the disciples fell at his feet trembling, he lifted them with the words: "Fear not!" When their ship was sinking in the storm, they heard the assuring words, "Fear not!" When he was leaving them, he comforted them, saying: "Let not your heart be troubled." (Jn. 14:1). Are you afraid of your sins, do not be afraid: "The son of man has the power to forgive sins" (Mk. 2:10). Are you afraid of the devil, fear not, he has overcome the world and cast out the prince of this world (Jn. 12:31). Are you afraid of life's changes and uncertainties, fear not, all things are possible to him that believes (Matt. 19:26). Are you afraid of the future, fear not, little flock for your Father is pleased to give you the kingdom" (Lk. 12;32). So, with Jesus, we can march boldly into God's presence with assurance and confidence in his all-sufficient provision, knowing that the Lord has our well-being at heart. This way, we live in joy and hope that keeps us living out our vocation gracefully despite the odds. This is possible because the Spirit-animated joy can never be destroyed by persecution (Col. 1:24), suffering (Rom. 5:3-4), trials (1 Pt. 1:6-7), sorrow (2 Cor. 6:10), or sentence of death (Phil. 1:21). It is the hope of this joy set before us that helps us, like Jesus, to endure all manner of trials, suffering, and death (Heb. 12:2).

REALIZING THE JOY OF THE LORD

Joy in the believer is born the day he is baptized and receives the Spirit of the living God. The Spirit brings it as one of his many fruits, and with this, a new life is launched. This new identity in Christ is full of the joy of the Lord. Speaking about this, Jesus tells his disciples that our experience of the Holy Spirit would be like having "rivers of living water" within us (Jn. 7:38:39). He is the indwelling wellspring of joy in the Lord that we experience as we live by faith in the Son of God" (Gal. 2:20). Sequel to this, Paul teaches that we have the grace that makes us rejoice because God's love has been poured into our hearts through the Holy Spirit who has been given us (Rom. 5:2,5). That is to say that we already have the potential for river-like joy. Though bequeathed with joy through Christian baptism, it may remain latent in some Christians, waiting to be exercised. Then as we avail ourselves to the things of God, meditating on the word, praying, singing, and exercising the gifts of the Holy Spirit, we keep alive the joy of the Lord. In other words, as we begin to know God, abide in Christ, and walk by the Spirit, who fills and refills us when we are weary, gladness and joy will sweep our hearts and become our way of living. We are also to heed Paul, who teaches us to fan into flame the gifts of the Holy Spirit.

We are to do this by removing worldly things that may stand in the way of the Spirit or fan him into flame through the life of prayer, worship, adoration, and daily meditation on the Word. As long as the flame of the fire of the Holy Spirit is burning brightly, so will the steam of the river of joy in the Christian.

As a gift of the Holy Spirit, Christian joy is most caused and felt as a response to conversion. A transformed life is a joyful life. This is so because repentance liberates the sinner from the bondage of sin and guilt. The guilt of sin keeps the heart and mind restless and robs the sinner of peace and joy. When life changes through repentance, it helps the person to experience a deep sense of freedom and gladness as he enters an intimate relationship with the Lord. Because repentance disposes a person to embrace and realize the place of Jesus as Lord, his new life carries a deep feeling of peace and joy. In this way, joy becomes the result of the believer's response to God's saving activity. This new life of grace makes the believer exude joy. In other words, joy is a feeling that is cultivated when we make Jesus the Lord of our life. When this happens, it carries a feeling of assurance, security, and certainty. Alan Jackson captures it well in his hymn:

Blessed assurance, Jesus is mine!
Oh, what a foretaste of glory divine!
Heir of salvation, purchase of God.
Born of his Spirit, washed in His blood.
This is my story, this is my song.
Praising my Savior all the day long
This is my story; this is my song.
Praising my Savior all the day long

by Fanny Crosby, 1873

According to this hymn, a certain feeling of assurance of the Lord's presence brings a foretaste of divine glory but not without the spring of joy. Often such experience finds expression in singing and praising, smiling and jubilation. One finds himself in a euphoric state of being with a heart basking in joy, confidence, and hopefulness. It may begin with a mere feeling of appreciation of God's goodness or desire for his presence: "I am happy when they say let us go to the house of God" (Ps. 122:1).

Because the Holy Spirit, whose fruit is joy, animates all our sacramental celebrations, as such, every celebration of the saving work of the Lord is an opportunity to renew joy. The angelic joy of the birth of Jesus is still with us. Though the forces of evil seem to be everywhere, the good news that the savior is born for our salvation is a joy. It is a joy that neither pain nor sorrow can diminish, and neither hunger nor intimidation from human authorities can take away. In Jesus is our Good News; we celebrate God's availability to his people; the invisible God is made visible to us. Jesus does not only become one of us to reveal the Father; he makes God easily accessible to each one of us. He became man so that man in his human condition can reach God and have a relationship. In other words, salvation history did not end with Jesus's coming; it continues into our day. Sometime today, and every other day, God comes; God is with us, and the joy is ours to celebrate. As Paul puts it, the implication of this is that each of us now has the opportunity to be saved (2 Cor. 6:3). In fact, with the birth of Jesus, our Good News, God is not only with us but for us. Even today, we still celebrate his ever-present presence in the Eucharist, a great source of joy. In the Mass, we celebrate a joy that comes from the conviction that God loves us, forgives our sins, and dwells within us. It is the joy of Jesus Christ himself made present in our hearts through the Holy Spirit who dwells within us (Rom. 5:2-5). He is here to fight our battle in our darkest moments. This is a priceless assurance and good news that calls for relish and joy.

The resurrection of the Lord is another source of joy for Christians of all time. Jesus came to redeem humanity but was greeted with death. Before his death, Jesus told his disciples that he would be raised after three days. "Let these words sink into your ears; for the Son of man is to be delivered into the hands of men" (Lk. 9:44). When he died, it was a disaster, and every disciple was in agony. There was great joy amongst the disciples when Jesus rose triumphantly from the dead. They were joyful that their hopes were not broken but fulfilled, a joy that their future was not destroyed but perfected. As such, their life was not in danger but secured for all eternity. The same joy is present among Christians of all ages whenever we think of or celebrate the resurrection.

When we have a good relationship with the resurrected Jesus, we can always rejoice in the Lord. Because there is joy in the Lord, joy becomes a way of living when we have a relationship with him. Christian joy, therefore, is born from knowing we are God's children. The cheerfulness that comes from this kind of relationship is a necessary consequence of our divine filiation that God loves us with an everlasting love and is constant in his affection for us (Jer. 31:3). The belief that I have God or that he takes care of me is not only a saving grace but brings healing and divine security. The divine security we feel as sons and daughters of God floods our hearts with joy. It is the joy of having been chosen and saved by Jesus, who still accompanies us. This belongingness brings a pleasant feeling and elicits cheers and delight. It is this relationship the psalmist has in mind when he says: "I rejoice in the Lord for he has clothed me with the robe of salvation and mantle of justice. If the psalmist believes and declares thus about joy, you and I have more reason to rejoice because we are clothed on the day of our baptism with the garment of salvation and indwelt with the Spirit whose fruit is joy. Like the psalmist, we rejoice in our salvation (Ps. 51:12), and he will never leave us. We rejoice because the Lord, the Mighty Savior is in our midst. In him, we "Cry out with joy and gladness, for among us is the great and Holy One of Israel" (Is. 12:6).

So, in the Lord, the Christian has an eternal connection, and while on earth, we experience the foretaste of the joy that will eclipse believers at the end of time. This everlasting dimension of joy awaits believers. One day we will stand before him and hear him say: "Well done, good and faithful servant; you were faithful over a few things; I will make you ruler over many things. Enter into the joy of your lord" (Matt. 25:21). Eternal joy of the Lord awaits believers who serve God faithfully. For now, this joy involves faith. As Peter puts it: "Although you have not seen him, you love him, and even though you do not see him now, you believe in him and rejoice with an indescribable and glorious joy, for you are receiving the outcome of your faith, the salvation of your souls" (1 Pt. 1:8-9). This eternal joy will outlast death and only increase in us forever (Mk. 10:21). It is the hope of this eternal joy set before us, which we lay hold on by faith, and which makes us "more than conquerors" over any obstacle to the love of God in Christ Jesus (Rom. 8:37). Joy is the welcome word of the Master at the end of life. Joy is the life and manner of things in eternal glory. Heaven is full of joy (Lk. 15:6-7).

CONCLUSION

Joy is a river-like experience of conversion that floods the heart with delight and graciousness and leaves the believer basking in the euphoria of godly peace, love, harmony, confidence, and hope. As a spiritual stirring and an intuitive sense of being enlivened and enlightened that is orchestrated by the Lord, every Christian who encounters the presence of the Lord experiences it. Our hearts are stirred with joy at the presence of the Lord when we surrender and allow him to have his way in our lives and possessions. Thus, joy brings about a state of being that is experienced, transforming, sustaining, living, and life-giving. Is it any wonder Mother Teresa sees joy as the "result of a heart burning with love," while Pope Francis sees it as "the air which Christians breathe?"

Because joy is the air of the Christian religion burning with love, Paul exhorts Christians to rejoice in the Lord always and again, I will say it again (Phil. 4:4). Unfortunately, our daily experiences reveal that life is not always lived on the mountaintop where everything is clear, goals are achieved, accomplishments noted and faith easy. Instead, life is generally lived not in cities and upstairs but in the valleys where you get up and go to work every day, and where you wonder at the end of the day what it was all about, and where faith is tested and tried, and struggles falter. But no matter which situation we find ourselves in, Nehemiah tells us to allow the joy of the Lord to be our strength (Nehemiah 8:10). The world needs the strength that comes from the joy of the Lord.

Though the New Testament letters are full of commands for Christians to be joyful and not give in to worries, joy is not enough to be known as a word or even commanded; every Christian should strive for a joyful heart. A joyful heart is one that delights in goodness and appreciates the value of what is right and just. It is a heart that thinks of whatsoever things are true, whatsoever things are honest, whatsoever things are just, whatsoever things are pure, whatsoever things are lovely, whatsoever things are of good report, virtuous, and praiseworthy (Phil. 4:8). It is a heart that delights to be cheerful, rejoices at right and expresses gratitude for small deeds and big deeds. It is the heart of a person who puts his trust in God and keeps his eyes on the good in every situation. Because his life is one of constant attitude born of faith in Christ who loves us (1 Jn. 4:16), he is grateful and gracious in all situations. Dispositions of this kind are the ingredients for which the Christian life is known and can never be present in any heart without an incessant surge of joy, gladness, and cheerfulness.

In fact, there are several ways of being filled with joy, as there are many ways of encountering God. The challenge is that if we wish to experience the joy of salvation continuously, we should keep open all the emotional doors of our lives for him to enter and inhabit. This is so because it depends on the human person to dispose of oneself to the divine. It is in view of this mystery of the divine-human receptivity that John goes on to say: "He came to what was his own, but his own people did not accept him. But to those who did accept him he gave the power to become children of God, to those who believe in his name" (Jn. 1:12). We are to accept that though he is accessible, yet he demands our acceptance, our conversion, our trust and worship, and our willingness to be faithful disciples. All we need do now is to seek to understand the Savior's Presence among us and how he works in everything for our well-being. What we already know about him may be little, but we have the capacity to know more as we draw near to him, Jesus, our Good News! When this is done, we cannot but live always in joy.

We are, therefore, to feed our lives daily with the word of God to enlarge our hearts with grace and fill it with divine insight and nourishment. The Christian message has as its aim to lead us into communion with God so that *our joy may be complete* (1 Jn. 1:4). This is important because the word of God has the power to flood the heart and mind with joy and gladness. We are also to fan into flame the Spirit of God we received on the day of our baptism to fill our lives with the joy of his presence constantly. As the Lord comes our way each passing day through his Word and Spirit, so is our joy and gladness.

Christians should seek and provide for joy because it does not benefit the joyful only but infects others. When we create a culture of life of joy, people who come in contact with us will feel the aroma of our gladness. Because the joy of the Lord is infectious, it has the power to spread from person to person. Just like Mary caused joy in Elizabeth and John with her greetings, we are to infect others with Christian joy. This means that when filled with joy, we become channels of God's grace and, like Mary, bring the presence of Jesus to those we meet, allowing the joy of the Lord to continue to spread.

Therefore, every Christian should endeavor to live a joyful life. Believers can always be energized by making a joyful noise and singing praises to the Lord after the example of David (Ps. 98:4). Our profession of faith demands us to rejoice and exult with our hearts to the Lord in all circumstances. Today, much more than any time, the words of Zephaniah are addressed to us: "Shout for joy, and Sing joyfully. Be glad and exult with all your heart. If not for anything, just because Jesus has redeemed us, God has begotten us and made us his heirs, and the Holy Spirit indwells us.

ABOUT THE AUTHOR

*F*ather Cletus Chukwudi Imo is a priest of Ahiara Diocese in Mbaise, Imo State, Nigeria. As a priest, he has served as a Formator and Dean of Seminary, Vocations Director, Chaplain of Catechists and Religious Education, Founder of Missionaries of the Lamb, and a Pastor. He is a theologian, educationist, school counselor, and pastoral counselor. He is currently the pastor of *St. John XXIII Catholic Community, Fontana/ Rialto, Diocese of San Bernardino, USA.*

Fr. Imo has spent decades working with young people and adults to discover and often recover their vocation, live authentic Christian lives and become missionary disciples. He has the eyes and heart of a good pastor. He believes strongly in the Scriptures as the power of God to save those who believe in Him (Rom 1:16) and selfless service to humanity motivated by love and compassion. He is also the author of *The Ministry of the Shepherd and the Church in Africa.*

www.ingramcontent.com/pod-product-compliance
Lightning Source LLC
Chambersburg PA
CBHW050449150626
46551CB00029B/2322